How to Sell Your Home

NOW

For the Best Price Possible

Mark Fields

How to Sell Your Home

NOW

For the Best Price Possible

Mark Fields

YAV PUBLICATIONS
ASHEVILLE, NORTH CAROLINA

First Edition

ISBN: 978-1-937449-50-6 paperback
ISBN: 978-1-937449-51-3 ebook
ISBN: 978-1-937449-56-8 audiobook

Published by

YAV PUBLICATIONS
ASHEVILLE, NORTH CAROLINA

Books may be purchased in bulk for educational, business, fundraising, or sales promotional use: contact Books@yav.com
For additional information:
Mark@MarkFields.com or phone 828-253-2491.
POB 2175, Asheville, NC 28802
Visit Mark's website: HowToSellYourHomeNow.us

Illustrations: Olga Poletavkina
Cover: Stojan Mihajlov

3 5 7 9 10 8 6 4

Published November 2021

Printed and Assembled in the United States of America

Dedication

This book is dedicated to my father Archie Fields
who instilled in me the value of hard work,
of working to be the best at everything I do,
and who demonstrated to me the infinite
power of effective marketing.

Acknowledgments

Thank you to Kristin, Bill, Linda, Chris, Keith, Edward, Greg, Olga, Stojan, Diane, Jerry, Ronnie, Allegra, and Jim for your support and contributions along the way!

CONTENTS

Foreword

It's common sense, but the 39 years I spent assisting thousands of clients as a consumer rights attorney drove home a central truth about selling your home: Ignorance is not bliss but instead is your greatest enemy, while knowledge and careful planning are the keys to maximizing your success. And, the best way I know to maximize your chances for success is to have the right guide, someone who knows how it all works—and who is truly dedicated to you and your success.

Someone like Mark Fields.

I've known Mark for many years and know that he is highly knowledgeable, experienced, hardworking, and dedicated to his clients. But what really sets Mark apart is his deep compassion and sense of public service. He doesn't think it's right that some have the benefit of a knowledgeable guide for selling their home, while others are left in the dark. To remedy that imbalance, Mark has written this book so that he can share his knowledge, expertise, and insights gleaned from more than forty years as a realtor to help you avoid the pitfalls and get the most you can from the sale of your home.

I hope and trust that you will find "How to Sell Your Home NOW" as informative and useful as I did, and wish you success in the sale of your home.

William J. Whalen
Attorney, retired

Introduction

When you face any major decision in your life, you need to be prepared. Selling your home is both significant and consequential. There's a large amount of money at stake. Wouldn't it be great if your closest friend happened to be a real estate expert who could walk you through the process and give you the inside track on everything pertaining to the sale of your home? You'd have a confidant who wouldn't be spinning information for their own benefit.

Allow me to be that confidant for you. I am an expert in real estate, here to make sure you are making the best decisions as you sell your home. Most of what I recommend in this book is not taught in real estate school.

My goal is to empower you, the seller, with knowledge, tools, and techniques that will ensure you get the best price for your home and sell it in the shortest time possible. I will guide you in what to do and what not to do to improve the value and appeal of your home to buyers, and I will teach you everything you need to know about marketing it. After reading this book, you will feel empowered and confident in navigating the successful sale of your home from start to finish, and I expect you'll enjoy the experience!

Mark Fields
April 24, 2021

Part One

FIRST STEPS

CHAPTER 1

You've Decided to Sell Your Home

If you are like most Americans, your home is your most valuable asset, and selling it is one of the biggest financial transactions you will undertake in your life. This can be a positive, exciting decision—the beginning of a new phase in your life—but it can also be stressful, because the decision involves more than just money. A home represents a chapter in your life, and moving always stirs up emotions.

Before you go any further, I want you to ask yourself a question: "Am I really, truly ready to sell my home now?"

This is a vitally important question, and you need to answer it honestly. If the answer is one hundred percent yes, terrific. That makes things easier. But don't be afraid to admit the truth to yourself. You may be sad to leave this home, considering all the memories you've made here. You may have invested time, money, and energy in making it beautiful in ways that only you appreciate. It's possible that even though you've decided to sell, you're not yet fully committed to taking the next steps.

If that's the case for you, please turn to the chapter "Energy, Intention, and Intuition" for suggestions about coming to terms with the decision to sell. I don't want you to list your home and have it sit on the market for months, while you get it ready for showing after showing, with all of this work leading to nothing because in your heart you are not ready to let your home go. Trust me, buyers will feel that—and it will turn them away.

But let's say you are ready to sell. You're excited to realize the value of your biggest asset and move on to the next phase of your life. This book will help you maximize your profit and minimize your stress. In the forthcoming pages, I will show you how to:

☞ Sell your home for the highest price possible
☞ Sell your home as quickly possible
☞ Be empowered by the experience

Perhaps you're thinking of handling the sale yourself. Do you know the demands and the pitfalls? Are you confident you will come out ahead at the end of the process?

Realtor™

"Realtor (TM)" is the trademarked term owned by the National Association of Realtors (NAR) referring to a Real Estate Agent or Broker who is a member of their organization. Even though it has become commonplace for the public to use the term Realtor when referring to a Real Estate professional, for the purpose of this book we will not use the term "Realtor" so as not to infringe on the NAR's trademark. We will instead refer to Real Estate professionals as a Broker or an Agent. The terms Qualifying Broker, Broker-In-Charge, and Managing Broker (these titles change from state to state) refer to the person responsible to the state real estate commission for the actions of their office and its agents. They are also responsible for the training and supervision of the agents in that office.

More likely, you've decided to list your home with a local real estate agent. But do you know how to choose the right one? Most people choose a real estate agent after doing little research or none. They ask the agent what the property is worth, and in most cases, blindly accept the real estate agent's figure. They sign a one-year contract, abandon all oversight of the agent's work, and just hope for the best.

All real estate agents are not the same. Hiring just any real estate agent can be a costly mistake.

In real estate, as in every business, there are great, good, decent, and bad professionals. When you don't know what to expect from a real estate broker, or how to go about choosing one, it's a roll of the dice. Unfortunately, the chances of ending up with a terrific real estate broker are probably less than the chances of rolling an eleven. You've probably been to a party where the conversation turned to property sales and heard horror stories. Almost everybody has at least one. An awful lot about the real estate profession isn't taught in real estate school.

You can avoid most negative experiences if you understand the process. The real estate world can be complex, but as a seller, what you need to know is not rocket science. I will share with you the most effective strategies, and best practices, for selling a home—knowledge that will empower you to interview and hire a great real estate broker, and be able to assess at all times whether they are doing their job to the highest standard. I want you to know how to price your home correctly. I want you to know what to demand of the professional you are paying the big bucks to represent you.

Commission

When you hire a real estate agent, you will pay out a substantial sum of money for their work. If the sale price of your home is $500,000, the agent's commission, at the usual figure of 6%, will be $30,000. That is a lot of money.

The standard commission paid to real estate brokers for their services varies by locality and according to the type of property and the level of services provided. Though there are no set rules, "full service" brokers usually receive a commission of 6% of the final sale price on sales of residential property. For empty lots or raw land such as farms, 10% is the most common commission.

Whatever the sale price of your home, 6% of it represents a lot of money. Don't you think you should receive maximum value when paying that much for a service?

Most people think of the real estate agent's commission as merely a necessary cost of the sale, not as money they are actually paying for services. This is because sellers never really receive that money, since it is deducted by the attorney or escrow agent from the money paid by the buyer, and transferred to the agent directly as an expense of the transaction. You don't write a check to the real estate agent, so it doesn't feel like this is money you are actually spending—but I assure you, it is.

Considering the broker's commission as a fixed cost rather than a purchasing decision is a mistake—and can be a costly one.

If sellers had to pay their real estate broker even half of the 6% commission up front, when signing the listing agreement, they would be much more diligent in choosing their broker, and I probably would not be writing this book. I urge you to think of the agent's commission as money you are actually spending. This book will guide you in spending it wisely.

CHAPTER 2

Do You Really Need a Real Estate Agent?

Most of us are always on the lookout for ways to save money, and not paying that hefty commission might seem like a great opportunity to maximize your profit. You may think, "How difficult can it be? I put a 'For Sale' sign in front of my house, place an ad in the paper, blast it on social media, and wait for the phone to ring. Voilà!" But if it really was that easy, everybody would be doing it, and the real estate profession would not exist.

Maybe you're thinking that you cannot afford to pay 6% off the top of the sale, because then you won't have enough money to pay off your mortgage, or whatever you may need the money for. This is a different economy—I will show you why.

Before you commit to embark on the sale of your home yourself, consider these questions:

- ❷ Do I really understand enough about the process to handle the sale myself?
- ❷ How much money will I actually save?
- ❷ Might I actually end up with less money by trying to save money?

Put yourself in the buyer's shoes

You're looking for a buyer, so the best way to attract one is to understand their priorities and their likely strategies. It's like fishing. You don't just throw a hook into the water. You bait it with something the fish will want to eat, and you go to a place where you believe the fish are.

MLS

An MLS, or Multiple Listing Service, is a private database that is created, maintained, and paid for by real estate professionals to help their clients buy and sell property. In most cases, participating brokers provide access to MLS listings information to their clients free of charge.

So, imagine that you are the one looking to buy a home. Do you cruise the streets looking for yard signs? Do you even know which streets to cruise? And do you do it again and again, day after day, week after week, down all the streets that appeal to you, looking for what's new on the market?

Maybe some people have the time and inclination to do this. More likely, you're busy at your job, making the money that you will use to buy your next home.

If you are like most people today, you will search online. There are many websites that provide search services for people looking to purchase, sell, or lease real estate; these include Zillow.com, Trulia.com, and Realtor.com. When a real estate agent lists a home and posts it on their local MLS (Multiple Listing Service), in most instances, the listing is immediately shared with these online real estate search engines.

When you find a home that you like, you will want to see it, and to do that you will need to find an agent to show it to you. Maybe you will choose the real estate agent who is representing that home or another one that you like the look of, or maybe you have a friend, or a friend of a friend who is an agent, or maybe you'll just walk into a local real estate office. You'll ask the agent to show you the properties you found online, and you may ask them to also show you other available properties that meet your specifications.

This is why most buyers arrive with a real estate broker representing them. And when that professional brings a buyer to your home, they will expect to be paid half of the total commission—commonly 3% of the sale price.

The commission

Let's continue with the previous situation, but now you've put your own shoes back on: you are the seller and you've got an offer—from a buyer who has viewed your property with the help of a broker. You've decided not to use a real estate agent because you don't want to pay the commission. You could, in theory, refuse to pay the buyer's broker their usual commission, or try to negotiate the amount of the commission down. If you do, what do you think that broker's next move will be? They'll point their client toward a different property. This is perfectly reasonable. The broker has put in time and effort for their client, so why would they want to spend even more time negotiating with you and not get paid?

"Aha," you may think, "I'll demand that the buyer pay their broker directly." But think about it for a moment: in the end, that won't make any difference. The buyer has a sum of money they are willing to pay, and it doesn't matter to them whether they pay it to you or to their broker. If they're paying it to their broker, it's not going into your bank account. No matter how the paperwork is done, 3% of the money that changes hands will go to the buyer's broker rather than to you.

What about the other half of the commission?

"Okay," you think, "I'll agree to pay the buyer's broker's half of the commission. At least I save the other half." That's 3%, which in our earlier example of a $500,000 sale price amounts to $15,000. That's still a lot of money.

But will you save that entire half of the commission?

No. You will have expenses on the sale: signage, marketing materials (photography, websites, brochures), advertising. Your savings continue to diminish.

Consider the time you will need to invest, not to mention the stress involved. You must prepare all those marketing materials yourself and promote your listing. You'll probably have to put in time learning how to do both of those things, and you may discover you need to hire a graphic designer, since DIY (Do It Yourself) design often looks awful. Also, do you trust your own expertise enough to be sure you will create the most powerful website and other marketing materials? Once your house is on the market, potential buyers will want to see it, so you will have to be the one to show it, over and over—and, probably, over and over again, as you'll lose a sale here and there by saying the wrong thing or missing an appointment or a deadline.

Other Factors to Consider

Access to the Market

I mentioned the MLS earlier. You might find a local broker who will give you access to the MLS for a fee, or for a reduced commission at the time of sale. For a fee, some companies will help you advertise an FSBO (For Sale by Owner) property, and, for an additional cost, they may offer supporting services such as photography, signs, and printing. My experience, however, is that the quality of these services, with few exceptions, is significantly inferior to what an exceptional real estate broker can offer.

If you do navigate one of these alternate routes, you will expose your property to a larger audience of buyers than if you simply put up a sign and take out an ad in the local paper. But even that just isn't enough.

In order to reach the largest audience of buyers, your property must also be marketed to real estate professionals, because, as I explained, your potential buyers will come with an agent or other broker. If a real estate agent is representing your property, they will also market your home directly to the other agents in your area, which will increase the number of potential buyers. If you choose to sell your home yourself, you will not have access to this vitally important market.

Marketing

Many properties today are sold through the help of terrific marketing materials enhanced by professional photographs, an excellent property description, captivating printed brochures or cards, a video, a virtual tour, and a dedicated property website. You'll be competing against this, and without comparable marketing materials, your home will appear much less appealing. You can create such materials yourself (at some expense), but can you do it as skillfully as a professional with years of experience and daily knowledge of what the competition is doing? The process can get costly, since you will need to pay for photographs, graphic design, printing, website design, and programming. Plus, how are you going to let people know that your website even exists?

Negotiation and Legal Documents

As described previously, a poor negotiation can kill a deal, or leave you with much less money than you might have made on the sale of your home. But let's say you've come to an agreement on price and terms with a buyer. You're on your own, without an experienced, knowledgeable representative. Do you know what legal documents you, the seller, must produce, and will you really understand what you are signing? At the very least, you'll need an attorney to make sure you're not being swindled or making some terrible mistake.

A Final Check-in

If you're still thinking of going it alone, make sure you can answer "yes" to the following questions.

❷ Are you confident in your ability to correctly price your home—neither undervalued nor overvalued—in order to maximize your profit in your current market?

- Are your marketing skills strong enough to communicate your property effectively to potential buyers? This will include hiring a photographer and overseeing the photo shoot, creating an attractive brochure and property website, compiling all the most important information on your home for a buyer, and ensuring that real estate brokers in your market are aware of your property.
- Are you confident in your ability to prepare your home for market in a way that will maximize its appeal?
- Do you know how to ensure that your buyer's appraiser will give your home its highest valuation? (Low appraisals kill sales.)
- Are you a skilled negotiator?
- Do you know what legal documents you must bring to the table to enter into a contract for the sale of your home?
- Are you comfortable completing, reviewing, and signing the required legal documents on your own?
- Do you know the legally mandated disclosures required by a seller in your state?
- Are you aware of the state and federal laws governing fair and equal housing that can impact you as a seller?

If you answered "no" to any of these questions, you should definitely hire a skilled, professional broker, but first, you need to know how to choose the right real estate agent for your home.

CHAPTER 3

Choosing Your Agent

I hope I have convinced you that hiring an agent will maximize your profit and minimize your stress as you sell your home. Please do not think of what you are paying a real estate broker as a fixed cost of the sale. You are about to pay someone thousands, maybe tens of thousands, of dollars for a professional service. Even though you are not putting down any money now—in fact, it may never feel like you're spending that money at all—*never forget* that you are paying handsomely for the services you are about to contract. Don't hire your real estate broker casually.

▲ Don't just call a real estate agent friend.
▲ Don't just hire your friend's broker friend.
▲ Don't just act blindly on somebody's advice and hire their agent.
▲ Don't just hire the best-looking real estate agent with the glamorous photograph.
▲ Don't just get a real estate broker's name off the sign in front of a nearby house.
▲ Don't just walk into or call a local real estate office and take the first agent you meet.
▲ Don't just call one of the companies that advertise on TV promising to get you the top agent in your area or guaranteeing to sell your home in 30 days.

Take your time. Do your research. Find that highly skilled professional who will go the extra mile to ensure that you have the best possible chance of selling your home quickly and at the highest price possible.

When, after ten years working in real estate in Costa Rica, I moved back to the U.S. in 1988, I bought and sold many properties. Real estate was what I knew, having grown up working with my father, who was a real estate marketing master. As I did not yet have my U.S. real estate license, I had to use the services of a broker. My father taught me that, as a broker, you never want to arrive at a closing and feel that you haven't earned your commission, or have your client feel that way. Yet not once did I show up to a closing and feel good about paying the 6% commission. Heck, much of the time I couldn't even get the broker to return my phone calls, even on properties where they stood to earn over $100,000. Then, when I became a real estate broker, I discovered that many of my clients regarded real estate brokers in the way they regarded used car sales agents—as fast talkers and poor performers.

When I became a licensed broker and started servicing clients, while buying and selling properties myself, I resolved to set a higher standard. I set my personal goals high and always went the extra mile for my clients. With the help of this book, you can make sure your agent does the same for you.

As the seller, you are in charge. You have sole authority over the sale process. Even though you will sign a contract with a real estate broker, it is your home and your money. You are the boss! You have the right to choose how your home will be sold, and who will sell it for you. You have the right to negotiate all aspects of the contract with the agent. You have the right to hold the agent accountable, and the right to fire the real estate agent if you are unhappy with their performance.

But please remember: your contribution to the process is not over once you've chosen your real estate broker. Even the best broker can only do so much. In the end, it's up to you to create the conditions that will bring about the most advantageous sale.

Find the right agent for you

First, let's be clear about the difference between the real estate agent and the real estate company. Some brokers work alone; others associate themselves with companies that may be local or may have franchise offices around the world.

The individual agent is the one who manages your listing. Brokers have a great deal of autonomy, so two properties being handled by the same company may be marketed with vastly different levels of skill. The company provides legal and marketing support, such as help with paperwork, templates for brochures, graphic designers, videographers, and people who will measure a home and create a floor plan. It also provides an office, a receptionist, and a telephone system—which may become less important as things move online.

Many people are under the impression that listing their home with a giant company gives them an advantage, since people in Paris or Shanghai will see their listing. This isn't so. Imagine that person in Shanghai looking through the glossy company magazine, and noticing your lovely home in Austin, Texas. By an amazing fluke, they want to buy a property in Austin (or perhaps they're considering the entire region), but they haven't contacted any local real estate agents yet. They decide to visit Austin in July, and contact the agent to arrange a viewing. Almost certainly, they'll ask to view any other houses that fit their specifications as well—and the real estate broker will decide which houses to show them. So, it's far more important that your real estate broker has done a good job of marketing to other real estate agents in your area than whether your house appears in a magazine that's distributed in Paris and Shanghai.

It's the real estate agent who is going to do a good or bad job for you, not the company. Your goal is to find the agent who understands how to do the most powerful marketing job for your home. If they work with a financially well-resourced company, so much the better, but it's a long way down the priority list.

Three steps to find the best broker for you:

1 ▸ Research Local Real Estate Agents and Make a Shortlist

Online Search Engines

The most popular real estate search engines in the U.S. today are Realtor.com and Zillow.com. Go to one of these sites and enter the location of your home. Now, select a price range. If you've had an appraisal within the last two years, use that figure and a range of 20% lower and higher. If you haven't had an appraisal, search for properties that are similar to yours *that have sold* within the last 12 months (not just those currently on the market), and make a list of those that seem most comparable in neighborhood, home size, lot size, and number of bedrooms.

Now, look more closely at the properties on your list. Pretend you're a buyer. Which listings are the most inviting, inspiring you to want to know more about the property? The real estate brokers handling those homes *may* understand how to deliver a property to the market. Which listings look dreary and uninviting? Strike those agents off your list.

If you don't find any listings in your price range that impress you, look in a higher price range. Real estate agents will naturally make more effort for a higher-priced listing, and you want to see what they're capable of. That's what you're looking for: the best marketing a broker has to offer.

Now, assess the components of each listing. The main photo is vitally important; either it instantly inspires a buyer to want to know more, or it turns them off. Does the brief description of the home make you want to know more? If you like what the real estate broker has done so far, click through. Look at the other photos. Are you impressed? Read all the information provided. Are you intrigued? If you were a buyer, would you be motivated to schedule a time to see that property in person?

For high-priced properties, expect a link to a virtual tour, or to a custom website that gives more photographs and more detail. The photos should be comparable to what you might see in a magazine such as *Southern Living, Dwell,* or *Architectural Digest.* No matter what the price range of the property, photos should always be of professional quality and show the home at its best.

Make a note of what you liked most about each listing, and note the name and contact information of the agent on that listing. These real estate agents are, for now, your top choices—whatever they look like. Don't be swayed by the good-looking broker in the photo smiling up at you. A pretty face does not equal a good broker.

Price Ranges

For convenience, I will break these down.
High: in the top 10% of the price range in your area.
Medium-high: from 70% to 90% of the top price in your area.
Medium: from 30% to 70% of the top price in your area.
Low: in the bottom 30% of the price range in your area.

Local Real Estate Publications

Pick up the top real estate magazines and newspapers in your area. Jot down the contact information of the agents representing the most attractively presented properties in your price range and above.

Friends and Neighbors

A referral from a friend or neighbor, based on their personal experience, is an excellent reason for putting a real estate broker on your shortlist—though not a reason to hire them instantly! Ask your closest friends if they know of a top-notch real estate broker in your area and whether they base their recommendation on personal experience or the experience of someone they know. Ask neighbors who sold their home in the last year or so if they were pleased with the agent who represented them, and what qualities stood out to them.

Now you have your list, but your task is not finished! Please do not choose your real estate broker yet, however convinced you are that you've found the right one. Be patient. This is a vitally important decision, and you must make it with due care and attention. You're going to interview three real estate agents, so the next step is to decide which three they will be.

2 ▸ Research Your Top Six Candidates

Using your best judgment—and your intuition, too—select your top six candidates. Go to the website or company page of each candidate. Brokers often have their own individual websites, and if not, they will surely have a dedicated page on their company's website. Go to that company's website and look for a link titled "Our Agents" or "Our People" and search for the broker's name. You should then be able to find a link to "My Listings."

If you're having trouble finding a broker's listings, call them and tell them you're considering hiring them to sell your home and need a little more information. Ask them to send you their current and recent listings, with information about how long the property has been on the market, and examples of all their marketing materials, including materials that promote their listings to other real estate agents.

Review all their listings, and see if you think they are representing their clients well. Pay close attention to the quality of photographs, videos, virtual tours, and descriptions. Note how long these properties have been on the market; this information usually is found under the acronym DOM (days on market). This can be an indicator of two factors: whether the property is priced properly, and whether it has been brought to the market in the most effective way.

DOM

Days on Market
It is a widely held belief in the real estate profession that the longer your home is on the market, the less attractive it will appear to potential buyers. Buyers will think there must be something wrong with it, the thinking goes, or buyers will assume that the seller is vulnerable and willing to take a hit on the price.

Everyone wants to sell their home quickly, and sometimes, for different reasons, a property may take longer than other properties to sell. Intelligent buyers will not make assumptions when they see that a property has been on the market for a while; they will ask the seller's real estate agent why.

Don't fall into the trap of thinking that just because a home has been on the market for what you may feel is a significant amount of time, or for more time than most homes, the broker is not doing a good job. Many properties have idiosyncrasies. Perhaps that mountainside home has a pool, and people worry about how to deal with it in the winter, or perhaps the basketball court in the middle of another house turns buyers off. In many markets, high-end homes can average 600 DOM or more before they sell.

Read their client testimonials or reviews in the online search engines. Each time a real estate broker takes part in the sale of a property, representing either the buyer or the seller, they can receive an online review by their client. If a broker has five stars, that means they've probably never received a negative review. That's great—but it doesn't mean that if a candidate has only four stars, you should take them off your list. Some negative reviews are undeserved, and just one negative review will have a greater impact on the rating of a newer broker, who has fewer reviews, than on a broker with 100 reviews or more. Some top brokers have no reviews at all, because they don't need to solicit them. So read the reviews, but don't solely rely on them. Reviews are just one more source of information.

3 ▸ Interview Your Top Three Candidates

You are interviewing for the position of Executive Marketing Director for your property. You are not trying to convince these agents of anything. It's their job to convince *you* they are the right real estate agent for you.

Call your three top candidates and make a one-hour appointment with each of them, allowing at least half an hour between appointments in case they run over. Before you make the phone call, be prepared to provide the address of your home, the square footage, the size of your lot, the number of bedrooms and bathrooms, the age of your home, and whether your home has been updated since you purchased it. Tell the real estate broker that you plan to sell your home and you have chosen to interview them, among other brokers, because you like what you've seen of their marketing of other properties. Tell them up front, "I'm already confident in your ability to sell my home, but I want to get to know you better." Ask them to bring the names and phone numbers of three recent clients who would be open to speaking with you.

Notice How They Arrive at the Meeting.

Does it look like the broker cares about the impression their appearance will make on you? Are they dressed appropriately for the market, or are they overdressed (too fancy) or under-dressed (too casual)? In some markets, jeans are appropriate, as long as they are clean and matched with a tasteful shirt and sweater or jacket, expressing a casual elegance. If your home exudes formality, you might expect more formal dress. The real estate agent should have researched your home enough to know this prior to the interview.

As you greet the agent, notice fragrances or other smells. Perfume or aftershave can turn people off, so mellow or none is better. You don't know what will trigger someone negatively, but you can be pretty sure that body odor, pet smells, cigarettes, or alcohol will erode a buyer's confidence—as it will likely erode yours as well.

Prepare your home for this meeting as if you were going to show it to an interested buyer. It should be clean and tidy, looking its best. Give the real estate broker a tour of your home, then sit down for the interview. Decide in advance where you are going to do this. Choose somewhere comfortable with a surface on which the broker can display marketing materials, such as a coffee table in the living room or den, or the kitchen or dining room table.

Thank the real estate broker for coming, and remind them that you already know they do a good job, because you have done your research. Repeat that you are still deciding whom to hire, and you need a little more information. Be sure to get any documents that you requested, especially client testimonials and contact information for references.

Use the Interview Checklist in the next chapter to conduct the interview. Don't be surprised by the uncomfortable look on the broker's face as you go through the interview. Real estate agents are not accustomed to meeting with knowledgeable and empowered sellers. Some brokers feel that their great reputation precedes them, and they should not have to subject themselves to cross-examination. That is not your problem! You are interviewing for the best agent to represent *you*.

Take notes of the real estate agent's responses to your questions.

Interview Questions

❓ How long have you been a real estate agent?

❓ Why did you decide to become an agent?

❓ Do you like being a real estate agent? Why?

❓ What is your work background?

❓ Are you a member in good standing of the local real estate board?

❓ Have you ever had complaints filed against you to the local real estate board?

❓ Once you list a property, is it immediately available to everyone on the MLS or does your company hold it in-house for a time?

❓ Will you use a professional photographer or take the photos yourself?

❓ Will you make a video? If so, do you use a videographer?

❓ Do you create a website for each listing?

❓ How do you market online? What real estate search engines do you use?

❓ How long is the listing contract for?

❓ Are you open to suggestions and feedback from me?

❓ What criteria will you use to establish the price of my home?

❓ How long should I expect my house to be on the market?

❓ If I call you and leave a message, can I expect to hear back from you within 24 hours?

❓ Will you pass on feedback from the buyer after each showing?

❓ What is your policy for staying in touch with your client?

❓ Will you help me get my property ready to show?

❓ Do you have a list of reliable contractors who can help me get my house ready for sale?

❓ If I list my house with you, will you agree to attach a marketing addendum to the listing agreement that defines all the things you are committing to do for me as my broker?

❓ What expectations will you have of me as your client?

❓ Will you or your representative be here for every showing? If so, are you willing to arrive 15–30 minutes early to make sure the house is ready to show?

❓ What is your standard commission?

❓ Is there anything else you'd like to share with me?

CHAPTER 4

Interview Checklist

How long have you been a real estate broker or agent?

Don't be afraid to hire an inexperienced real estate broker. Many new real estate agents are hungry and ready to work harder than average for you. They may be more flexible and open to new ideas, since they will not have bad habits in place. This will make them easier to work with. In a buyer's market, selling is more difficult, so look for a real estate agent who will be creative.

Why did you decide to become a real estate agent?

The answer to this question may not help you decide about the real estate broker's ability, but it will help you get to know them a little better. This is both a personal relationship and a professional one, and it will go more smoothly if the broker representing you has values and priorities that are in accordance with yours.

Do you like being a real estate agent? Why?

Don't just listen to the words. Do you feel the real estate broker's enthusiasm for their work? An agent who loves what they do will be more creative and more willing to go the extra mile.

What is your work background?

This gives you more insight into who this person is and how they got here. Experience in marketing or negotiation, whether or not in real estate, can make a big difference.

Are you a member in good standing of the local real estate board?

The answer should be yes. If it is not, ask them to tell you why. There might be a good reason. Sometimes an official record doesn't tell the entire story.

Have you ever had complaints filed against you to the local real estate board?

Here, too, give the broker the benefit of the doubt. Some people complain for strange reasons.

Once you list a property, is it immediately available to everyone on the MLS or does your company hold it in-house for a time?

Some companies attempt to keep new listings in-house for one to three months to keep the entire commission (buyer's side and seller's side) within the company. This does not serve you well. It violates a real estate agent's professional code of ethics, because it severely limits the number of buyers who will know that your property is for sale. Your property should be marketed to *all* brokers in your market immediately—not just those at a single company.

Choose an agent who puts your listing on the open market immediately and commits to sending a printed or emailed notification to all other local real estate brokers as soon as they post a new listing.

Will you use a professional photographer? Or will you take the photos yourself?

A good real estate agent will always use a professional photographer, no matter what the price of the property.

Will you make a video? If so, do you use a videographer?

If your home is in the medium price bracket or above, expect the broker to create a video tour. The cost-to-benefit ratio of a video tour is very high; this is a powerful tool which can be created for as little as $200. I will discuss the different types of videos on page 67.

Be sensitive to the fact that the value of the property you are selling affects the amount of time and money the broker will invest in marketing it. The higher the value of your home, the higher the commission and the more sophisticated the marketing should be.

Please show me the marketing materials you create for buyer clients and for marketing to other real estate brokers.

If you already have examples of these, don't bring them out. Let the broker show you what they've brought—even if you didn't ask them to bring anything. If they've brought nothing to show you, this shows a lack of professionalism. Allow the real estate agent to explain their approach to marketing materials and what they think would be best for your property.

Choose an agent who understands the effectiveness of marketing to other brokers. Ask them to show you examples of the email marketing pieces they send out when a new property goes on the market. They may have to go online to do this, or email examples to you later. This is usually a letter-sized e-flyer designed to print and pass along to potential buyers. It should have an appealing banner with a title that draws a buyer in; for example, "Oasis on 10 Gently Rolling Acres" or "Get Away to This Paradise," along with the neighborhood or city and state. The main photo should be enticing. The property description can be brief, since people don't like to read lots of words, but it should list the most important details. A few more photographs should give a sense of the home. The e-flyer should include just enough information that a buyer will say, "I want to see that!"

When it comes to materials for buyers, again, I believe less is more. Depending on the size and complexity of your home, a simple 2- to 4-page brochure, elegantly presented, is more powerful than a 6- to 12-page booklet. Buyers are looking at multiple properties and may not want to spend much time reading extensive marketing materials, so it's best to make a quick impact. If the agent produces a lengthy booklet and suggests something similar for your home, ask whether they would consent to work with you on creating something simpler. (See page 59 and following for more information on marketing materials.)

Do you create a website for each listing?

You should expect a real estate agent to create a dedicated website if your house is in the medium price bracket or above. (You'll find more information on dedicated property websites on page 65.) This isn't as expensive as it sounds. A simple, but very nice one can be built for under $300.

How do you market online? What real estate search engines do you use?

Studies show that well over 90% of home buyers in the U.S. begin their search online. Ask which sites are the most popular for your area. The real estate broker should know and have a profile on each site. The agent's company should also have a website that targets buyers searching in your area.

How long is the listing contract for?

As a broker, I don't like to sign for less than twelve months. I don't want to put a lot of money and effort into getting a property ready for market and have the client pull the listing from me in six months for reasons that would almost certainly be beyond my control. I always operate on the assumption that a client will see that I am doing an excellent job for them and will not want to leave. Clients do sometimes get impatient and want to change brokers, but it's important to me to know that when we enter into this relationship, both sides believe we are in it together to get the best possible result.

You are doing your homework to hire the best real estate broker for you, so be willing to commit. You might say something like, "As long as you're doing an outstanding job, I'm going to stay with you." You'll generate a lot more goodwill this way. If you expect your real estate agent to go the extra mile for you, be willing to go the extra mile for them.

Are you open to suggestions and feedback from me?

The answer will almost certainly be yes, but that's not the important thing. Notice the broker's body language and tone of voice. Do they look uncomfortable as they say, "Yes, of course I'll listen to you"? Trust your instincts. Did you believe them? It's important to be able to express disagreement and offer suggestions without the agent getting defensive. By the time you've finished reading this book, you may have more ideas on how best to bring your house to the market than the real estate agent does. That's fine, if the real estate broker will listen and learn.

What criteria will you use to establish the price of my home?

This is a learning moment for you. The right price is established not only by considering recent sales of similar properties but also by an assessment of whether the price is competitive with comparable properties on the market right now. As I will explain later, the real estate market is always in flux, and only a broker who is on top of current trends can guide you effectively.

How long should I expect my house to be on the market?

In answering this, the real estate agent will discuss the DOM (days on market) of comparable properties recently sold and currently for sale in your area and price range. Typically, in most markets, the higher the price of a property, the longer it takes to sell.

If I call you and leave a message, can I expect to hear from you within 24 hours?

"Yes" is the correct answer. There is nothing more frustrating than calling your broker and leaving a message and not getting a return call. I find it extremely disrespectful. It makes you wonder: if they're not answering your phone calls or emails, are they responding to the buyer's broker who is trying to set up an appointment? Not taking the trouble to respond promptly is a sign of someone who doesn't care—especially when you consider how much money you are paying them to represent you.

Will you pass on feedback from the buyer after each showing?

Most MLS's email the buyer's broker immediately after every showing, asking them to rate it. Typically, the email asks for the buyer's level of interest, their opinion of the property, their opinion of the price, and any other comments they'd like to share. A good broker will usually complete this questionnaire within 24 hours of a showing, at which point your real estate agent will receive it.

What is your policy for staying in touch with your client?

You should expect a meeting or conference call **at least** once a month, in which your agent will update you on:

- The state of the market
- What comparable properties have sold in your area
- How many times they have shown your property
- Suggestions on what to do going forward

If they do not specify monthly or more frequently, ask if they will commit to such a time frame. Again, notice their body language and tone of voice as they respond.

Will you help me get my property ready to show?

Look for an answer like, "Absolutely! We will walk through your property with you and make a list of what needs to be done, on both the outside and the inside, to get it ready for market." Ask them if they noticed anything during the brief tour of your home you just gave them—this will help you assess whether they have an eye for detail. Do not expect them to conduct the detailed walk-through today; this is one of the services you are paying for if you hire them.

This is the time to prepare yourself to receive constructive criticism. You may not like what you hear, but it's far better to hear it now from someone who is on your side, than later, from a potential buyer trying to knock down the price or not making an offer at all. Don't argue! This is useful information. Take it seriously.

Do you have a list of reliable contractors who can help me get my house ready for sale?

Real estate professionals are in constant contact with service professionals. You may have your own go-to people, but this is a resource that an experienced real estate broker can offer you.

If I list my house with you, will you agree to attach a marketing addendum to the listing agreement that defines all the things you are committing to do for me as my broker?

Some real estate brokers may not be able to agree to this without checking their company policy, but they should be able to get back to you within 24 hours. See my Sample Marketing Addendum at HowToSellYourHomeNow.us. If they cannot provide the addendum, a letter or email outlining the services they are committing to will suffice.

What expectations will you have of me as your client?

This gives the real estate agent an opportunity to share with you how they like to do business. Look for confidence and clarity, but not rigidity.

Will you or your representative be here for every showing? If so, are you willing to arrive 15–30 minutes early to make sure the house is ready to show?

You can expect that the potential buyer's broker will accompany their client, and often this is adequate. But your house may have special features that only your broker can show effectively. A buyer's broker may not know to point out the radiant-heated black walnut floors, or the beautiful crown molding with discreet recessed lighting.

The seller's broker should always be present for showings of complex or unique properties and luxury homes.

If your agent arrives early, he can check that all the lights are on, clothing is put away, the kitchen is clean and tidy—whatever it takes to present the best impression. I once arrived for a showing of a $750,000 house and noticed spiderwebs in the windows. I found a rag, removed the screens, got rid of the spiderwebs, and replaced the screens before the potential buyer arrived. It was easy enough, but I couldn't have done it if I hadn't allowed the extra time.

What is your standard commission?

A broker's commission on a residential property typically ranges from 5% to 7%. For raw land or a lot without a house on it, the average commission is 8% to 10%. Ask whether the commission is negotiable; you don't want to discover later that the broker gave a discount to someone else and charged you the full amount. Some brokers are accustomed to giving discounts, others are not. Some company policies prohibit their brokers from negotiating on the commission. When someone asks me if my fee is negotiable, I usually say that it is not, because I will make a significant up-front investment in marketing, and I know that, when the property sells, I will have earned my fee.

Is there anything else you'd like to share with me?

This is a good way to wrap it up.

When the interview is over, walk the broker to their car. How well kept is it? Peek inside. Does it make a good impression on you, their potential client? Someone who does not spend money on a brand-new car every year may simply be thrifty—but is the car clean, and in good shape? Would a potential buyer be impressed and comfortable riding in it? This is more information for you as you consider who to hire to represent you.

Assessing the Interview

Now take some time to assess the interview:

- ❓ Did you like their answers?
- ❓ Are they enthusiastic about representing you?
- ❓ Did you like how they present themselves?
- ❓ Was communication easy?
- ❓ Do they appreciate what's most appealing about your home?
- ❓ Are you confident they will do what they say they will do? How confident?
- ❓ Do you feel good about entering into a long-term business relationship with this person?
- ❓ Were you impressed by their marketing materials?
- ❓ Were you physically attracted to this person? If so, do not let that drive your decision!

After you've interviewed all three candidates, review your notes and check in with your gut feeling about which broker will do the best job for you.

If you can't find someone who ticks every box, choose someone who is enthusiastic, keen to learn, and willing to go the extra mile. Choose someone you feel good being around. Choose someone who brings joy and excitement to the process of selling your home. If each of these first three candidates failed your assessment, go through this process with the other three brokers on your shortlist of six. That said, I bet you've found the right broker to represent you already.

The Listing Agreement

The listing agreement, often titled "Exclusive Right to Sell Listing Agreement," is usually a standard document created or approved by the state real estate commission. The terms of the document vary from state to state. Your broker will prepare this agreement for your signature. Take time to review it. It is a binding legal contract. Always know what you're signing.

Pay close attention to the following items:

1. **"Seller."** Make sure that the name given for "Seller" is the legal owner of your property. If this is you, has the real estate agent entered your full legal name? Do you own the property jointly with a spouse or someone else? If a trust or LLC owns the property, make sure it is designated as "Seller."
2. **Property Identification.** Double-check that the address is correct and that the PIN (Property ID) is correct.
3. **Term.** Does the term (or duration) of the agreement reflect your discussions with the real estate broker? The normal term in most markets is one year. Especially when the real estate broker is making a significant investment in marketing, it is only fair to allow time for their work to pay off.
4. **Termination.** As an agent myself, I always include a clause giving sellers the ability to end our listing agreement at any time, based on my belief that if I am doing a good job for them, they will want to keep my services. If your real estate agent doesn't offer this clause and you would like it included, your broker may request that you compensate them for their investment in marketing if you terminate the listing before

the term is up. Some brokers' companies will not agree to this.

5. **Taking Your Home Off the Market.** Perhaps your financial situation has changed, or you didn't get that job in another city that you thought was yours. You've decided not to sell after all. In addition to the marketing costs, you could be on the hook for the broker's commission if they have found you a buyer who meets all your terms with no negotiation, and you reject that offer. This is a very unlikely scenario, but be aware of it. Your real estate attorney can give you advice here.

6. **Fixtures.** The word "fixtures" refers to anything attached to the structure of your home. Chandeliers, wall sconces, curtains or blinds, and fixed TV brackets are all considered fixtures (the television itself is not, even if mounted to the wall). Fixtures are legally part of your home, and therefore as part of the sale, unless otherwise indicated. If there are fixtures you want to keep, identify them clearly (e.g., "chandelier over dining room table," "all light fixtures," "master bedroom curtains," "all window treatments") and specify in the listing agreement that they are "Not Included."

7. **Items Included in the Sale.** All such items should be listed individually. All kitchen appliances and washer and dryer are standard inclusions. (If you are not including certain appliances, be sure these are listed as "Not Included.") Specify any further items of value that you would like to pass on to the new owner, such as a whole house sound system, outdoor grill, patio furniture, or lawn mower.

8. **Listing Price.** Make sure this is the figure you have agreed on. This is the place to mention if you are open to owner-financing or if you require

payment in full (which in most cases means the buyer will have to secure a loan).

9. **Commission.** This should be the figure you agreed upon, with half going to your broker and half going to the buyer's broker.

10. **Existing Mortgages or Liens.** Most listing agreements require that you disclose any loans for which your home is serving as collateral. Be accurate.

11. **The Broker's Role.** Many states require that brokers formally disclose whether they are serving in this transaction as a seller's representative, a buyer's representative, or as a dual agent.

If the broker represents only one party (buyer or seller) in the transaction:

The broker is legally bound to serve your best interests, which includes following your lawful instructions, providing you with any information that could influence your decision-making, exercising care and diligence, and accounting for all monies handled on your behalf. Once the listing agreement has been signed, a seller's representative is forbidden to share any confidential information with potential buyers/sellers, unless you specifically give them permission to do so.

If the broker is representing both parties in the transaction (referred to as "dual agency"):

This can refer either to the real estate broker personally, or to the real estate brokerage with whom they are affiliated. Since there is a potential conflict of interest, this is something to which you must specifically agree, and you should insist on a clause forbidding the real estate agent to share confidential information with the other party in the transaction. In the case of a dual agency, the agent is legally bound to treat both parties fairly and equally, and owes them the duties as described above. There is also an arrangement known as "designated agency," which assigns different agents in the same firm to represent buyer and seller, thereby giving each side an advocate.

Marketing Addendum

Throughout the book I discuss the Marketing Addendum. You create accountability when you specify exactly what you expect your real estate broker to do in marketing your home. If you have agreed on one, make sure a Marketing Addendum is included.

Property Disclosure

This is a legal document in which you disclose detailed information about the property you are selling. Some states allow the seller to refuse to answer, or provide a box for "No Representation," meaning you choose not to disclose. Even if you are in one of those states, I recommend that you answer all the questions to the best of your knowledge. First, because it builds trust in potential buyers, and second, because if you hide a problem that is later discovered by the buyer's building inspection—as you should assume it will be—you could lose the sale. Be transparent and forthcoming.

Home Inspections

A home inspection is performed by a licensed home inspector and is normally done by the potential buyer after an offer is accepted. The inspector checks whether the home is in good condition, and may also inspect for moisture, mold, wood-destroying insects, fire damage, radon gas, water quality, the septic system, or anything else that might affect the value of the property.

If your current HVAC (Heating, Ventilation, and Air Conditioning) system is 30 years old, tell potential buyers here. If the roof is long past its expected life, tell them. If there's a leak in the roof, moisture in the basement, mildew, or any other serious problem, disclose it. Your buyer will discover these things anyway when they do their inspections. (More about inspections on page 81.)

Home Owners Association, Property Owners Association, and other covenants.

When selling your home, you must also disclose to potential buyers any information that may affect the cost of acquiring and owning it. If you are a member of an HOA (Home Owners or Property Owners Association), disclose any monthly or annual dues, as well as costs for transferring ownership and membership of the Home Owners Association or the POA (Property Owners Association). In addition to current and ongoing costs, disclose any special assessments approved by the Association that will cost the buyer additional expense in the future.

Prospective buyers will want to know the financial condition of the Association, and whether there are any pending legal actions that may affect it. Buyers often request a copy of the most recent financial statement and the minutes from the last two or three board meetings. You should also provide the name and contact information of the Association's board president and treasurer, and the name and contact information of the property manager and management company.

You should also disclose any restrictions on the use of the property. A Home Owners Association may have binding stipulations on renting the property or on pets. Other covenants may limit what kind of additions can be made to the building, whether any further buildings such as a guest house can be constructed, or, if there is extra acreage, whether you can subdivide. You don't want to waste your time and a potential buyer's time if any of these restrictions would be a deal-breaker.

Part Two

BRINGING YOUR HOME TO MARKET

The Eight Steps to Selling a Home

1. Pricing
2. Preparing your home for market
3. Marketing strategy and materials
4. Showing your home
5. Negotiating with the buyer
6. Inspections and disclosures
7. Legal documents
8. The closing

CHAPTER 5

Pricing

The first key to a successful sale is determining the proper asking price for your home. Many sellers price their homes too high. Of course, they want to get the most money possible—who doesn't? Often, they genuinely think their home is more valuable than it is.

Overpricing your home will keep many solid buyers away. But let's say someone comes to look at your home and likes it enough to want to make an offer. They will know what similar homes in your area are selling for, because they've probably looked at them, too, and they're unlikely to want to pay a premium for your home. The likelihood is that they won't make an offer at all. If they do, it will be in line with what they think the property is worth, not what you're asking. Result: you've drastically limited your pool of buyers, wasted your time showing your property to people who will soon see it's overpriced, and probably seriously increased the time your property spends on the market.

If you underprice your home, you will probably experience more interest and some offers. You can be pretty sure of making a sale, but at what cost? How much more money could you have gotten if you had priced your home correctly—even after you take 6% off the top?

A Story

Several years ago, I received a call from a homeowner who was interested in putting their property on the market. I scheduled an appointment, and after touring their beautiful home we sat in the living room to discuss how I would market their home. I told them that, based on my knowledge of the luxury market in their area, I would recommend a price between $1.1 and $1.25 million. A look of shock appeared on their faces. A few days earlier, they told me, they had met with a broker from one of the largest and most respected companies in the area, who had suggested a price no higher than $750,000. Then, I was shocked, too.

Just imagine: if they had trusted her professional opinion and put their home on the market at $750,000, it would have probably sold immediately for the full asking price, and they, not knowing any better, would have been impressed by what a great job she did. They might have never found out that they had lost several hundred thousand dollars on this seemingly successful sale. I can't tell you how many times I have heard stories like this.

Determining the Proper Price

Knowing how to price a home correctly takes experience and knowledge of current dynamics of the market in your area. Do you know whether prices are trending up or down? Do you know what kinds of properties are most in demand? Do you know what special factors are most important to current buyers? If you don't, you should get someone who does on your team.

Your real estate agent will make a recommendation based on research of the market, and will usually create a Comparative Market Analysis (CMA). Ask to see the research on which they base their figure. I always give my clients a range of prices, taking into account both the current market and how quickly they want or need their home to sell.

CMA

Comparative Market Analysis
A CMA is an assessment of a property's value based on recent sales in your market. Unlike an appraisal, which is done by a licensed appraiser, a CMA is created by a real estate professional.

Study the market yourself, and study your agent's report. Are you comfortable that they are judging the market correctly?

You and your broker will take into consideration many things when determining the asking price: square footage, number of bedrooms and baths, lot size, etc. Unusual features make a difference. Do you have a pool, a home theater, a two- or three-car garage? Do you have a wonderful view? Are you on a lake or oceanfront, or on a golf course?

Keep your expectations real. The higher your price, the fewer the number of potential buyers. Houses under $400,000 will attract more buyers than those priced between $500,000 and $600,000. When we hit the $1 million mark, the buyer pool in most markets shrinks dramatically.

If you're not in a hurry to sell, you might decide to start at a higher price, knowing that you can always drop the price later if necessary. But be careful of pricing your home so high that it's wildly uncompetitive with other properties of a comparable size and quality in the same or a comparable neighborhood. You'll alienate potential buyers, who will assume they'll get better value for money elsewhere, and may not even take the time to view your property in person. And if you do get a showing, it will likely be so that the buyer's broker can show their client what a great deal they're getting on the property right up the street or around the corner.

Remember, too, that the potential gain, if you achieve a higher price, is likely to be offset by the time your house spends on the market. Money itself has value. For example, let's say you have $100,000, which you invest in something that earns you 5% interest. If you have to wait a year before you get that $100,000, the wait has effectively cost you $5,000. If you'd priced your house at 95% of what you priced it at, you might end up with roughly the same amount of money and a year's less stress.

And that's if you sell it for your asking price after a year. In reality, houses that have been on the market for a long time rarely go for the full asking price. The buyer's real estate broker will use "days on market" to negotiate your price down—and at that point, your desperation to sell may lead you to agree to an even lower price than you might have gotten had you priced your home correctly to begin with.

On the other hand, if you underprice your home, you will surely get offers quickly, and you will sell your home, but at what cost? No one can answer that question accurately. You don't want to be the person who is delighted that they've sold their home quickly, then learns, six months later, that the buyer turned around and sold it for a handsome profit.

Get an Appraisal

If you don't have a recent appraisal on your home, now is a good time to obtain one. It will cost you some money, but an appraisal performed by a reputable local appraiser is a powerful tool in evaluating your real estate agent's suggestion for an asking price and defending that price when a buyer attempts to negotiate it down. A buyer can't expect that their mortgage lender will accept this appraisal, as lenders require their own appraisal, but if you attach your appraisal to your listing, the buyer's appraiser will see it.

Make sure your broker attaches the appraisal to your listing on the MLS.

A Buyer's Market vs. A Seller's Market

The real estate market is in constant flux. At one end is what we call a buyer's market; at the other end is a seller's market. Many factors influence these trends, and you may not be aware of all of them. It's unnecessary to go into them here—what matters is the relative number of buyers and sellers in a market.

In a buyer's market, the properties for sale far outnumber the buyers. Therefore, sellers are competing against one another to attract those buyers. Prices tumble.

Imagine there are 200 houses priced between $300,000 and $500,000 for sale in your neighborhood. If there are only twenty people looking to buy, 90% of the properties are going to stay on the market for an extended period. In fact, the proportion may be higher, as those twenty buyers may look in other neighborhoods as well. Once you, as a seller, have decided to sell, you don't want to wait for years. So it's in your interest to do everything you can to attract those buyers—and the most obvious thing to do is lower your price to make your price attractive.

Conversely, in a seller's market, there are more people looking to buy than there are houses for sale. Therefore, once a house goes on the market, it's likely to sell quickly and, if priced competitively, it may even receive multiple bids.

In a seller's market, your apparent need for a broker is diminished because you can probably find a buyer without help. Potential buyers are cruising the streets and they'll see your yard sign, even if you don't advertise in the paper. We don't see this type of market often, but when it happens, you can choose to do the transaction yourself—as long as getting the best price is not important to you and you are comfortable navigating all the legal contracts. In a seller's market, a property may well go for *more* than the asking price. A broker can solicit multiple bids and set deadlines, driving up the price. If you go it alone, the broker representing the buyer will take advantage of your lack of experience, and you, happy to have achieved a quick sale, will probably not even be aware of the money you're leaving on the table.

Adjusting the Price

If you believe that your property has presented well but you're not getting offers, quickly reassess. The cause may indicate a downturn of the economy, or it may be that this is a slow time of the year. Ask your broker whether your property is below average in number of showings, and don't accept a vague answer. You want hard information about the state of your local market. If you're getting an average number of showings but not receiving offers, price is most likely the problem.

If you're in a hurry to sell and other properties are moving but yours is not, consider dropping the price 3% to 5% after 30 days. The number of interested buyers should go up. If, after 60 days, the property still has not sold, drop the price by 3% to 5% again.

Continue to drop your price by 3%, 5%, or even 10% every 30 days until showings increase and offers come in.

An interesting situation may arise if you drop the price dramatically. Now your home really looks like a bargain, and often buyers will bid against one another. You might even get five or six offers within a day or two. An experienced broker can turn this into a mini-auction and edge the price back up.

CHAPTER 6

Preparing Your Home for Market

When potential buyers view your home, they carry in their minds an invisible checklist. As they arrive and look at the face of your home, the landscaping, the driveway, the neighborhood, and your neighbors, they are mentally checking positive boxes and negative ones. If they like the neighborhood, they check a positive box, if they like the look of your home's "face," they check another positive one. If the driveway, or condominium building, is in poor condition, they check a negative box. If the front door is worn or dirty, they check another negative box.

Each buyer has a threshold of how many negatives they'll accept before deciding, "No, I am not interested in this property." Every buyer's threshold is different, and some negatives are bigger than others. My goal is to guide you in doing everything possible to minimize the negatives. When a buyer leaves with very few negatives, your home will be on their "yes" list: "Yes, I like this home and I am considering buying it." That is where you want to be. The fewer the negatives, and the more the positives, the higher you are on the buyer's list.

If possible, continue living in your home while it is on the market. A property that is lived in—and kept show-ready, clean and organized—shows better and sells faster than a vacant one. Buyers like to imagine themselves living in a property, and that is much harder to do if the rooms are empty. If you cannot stay in your home, I strongly recommend that you hire a good staging company to furnish it for the time it is on the market.

Imagine you are a potential buyer. What will turn you on? What will turn you off? Go through your home, room by room, and make a list of everything you see that might turn off a buyer. Be honest. List everything; from major problems to trivial matters of clutter and dirt. Clutter and dirt make a home unappealing, no matter how wonderful it might be otherwise.

Here are some examples:

▲ The desk is disheveled and piled with papers.
▲ There are holes in the walls where we moved pictures or paintings.
▲ There are damp patches from a leak.
▲ The kitchen counters are crowded.
▲ The stove is greasy.
▲ There is a stain on the bedroom carpet.
▲ The kids' bathroom is a mess.
▲ The closets are crowded and disorganized.
▲ The bookshelves are cluttered and disorganized.
▲ The comforters on the beds are old and unattractive.
▲ The kitchen garbage can is full and smells unpleasant.
▲ The windows are dirty or scratched or fogged.
▲ The front door could use a coat of paint.
▲ The driveway is cracked and needs resurfacing.

Ask your agent to walk through the house with you and make recommendations. Add their recommendations to your list. Leave nothing off!

Put the time and energy into making your home look its very best. Not only will you increase the appeal of your home to potential buyers, you'll feel better while you're still living in it. I promise you it will pay off in the end.

In everything you do, aim for simple, neutral and elegant. A bookshelf should have plenty of books but should not be jam-packed, with books falling over. No surface should be cluttered with objects. Less is always better.

Repairs and Upgrades

It's vitally important to deal with anything that suggests a serious problem, even if that problem has already been fixed. Maybe you repaired the leak in the roof, but there's still a discolored patch of paint or wallpaper. That peeling paint on the window frame might mean the wood beneath is rotting.

When a buyer suspects that the owner of a property hasn't taken good care of it, they will become suspicious about what else might be wrong that they're not seeing. This puts you at a disadvantage. If a buyer sees enough things that concern them, they will walk away. If the buyer falls in love with other aspects of your property and decides to make an offer, you can expect it to be low and the negotiation to be tough. Conversely, when buyers see a home that is impeccably maintained, they perceive more value in the home and they are much more attracted to it.

Also consider whether you could make improvements to optimize the marketability of your home. Let's say the master bedroom closet is small. You instruct your broker to tell people that once the property is under contract, you'll build a big master closet. This is a dangerous strategy. Buyers are not good at envisioning changes, and they don't want to deal with repairs that might not be done well. Either they will try to knock far more than the cost of the closet off the asking price, or more likely they will keep on looking until they find a property with a good-sized master bedroom closet already in place.

Most buyers want a home that is ready for them. Unless a buyer is specifically looking for a fixer-upper, they tend not to be good at imagining possibilities. They are looking for something that fits their mental picture of what they want, and they will keep looking until they find it.

You may think, "Why should I spend money fixing this or changing that when I'm moving? I'll just let the new owner deal with it." The answer is simple: in almost every case, you will make back the money and more than what you invest in repairs and upgrades. And your home will sell faster.

Home Exterior and Landscaping

The first and last thing a buyer sees is the exterior of your home, your driveway, yard, and landscaping. First impressions are lasting ones, and so are last impressions. I have known people who flip homes and do nothing more than invest a few thousand dollars cleaning up the exterior and the landscaping before reselling the property for 10-20% more than they paid for it.

Remember the silent checklist the buyer has in their mind. You don't want negative check marks before the buyer has even set foot inside your home.

Roof

If your roof is looking worn, have a roofing company inspect it. If it is past its life span, the best thing to do is replace it. If you can't afford to do that, you still must know the cost of a new roof. Discount the purchase price by this amount and let the buyer replace the roof once they own the house. Offer a credit at closing for that amount.

Gutters

Visually, gutters are equivalent to the trim on your home. Dirty gutters give a negative impression. They suggest that your home is not well cared for. Pressure washing will not always clean them adequately, so you may need to get a ladder and a bucket of soapy water and clean them by hand or hire someone to do that.

Clean gutters inside and out. It's unnecessary to install leaf guards, as they are not visible from below, and I have never known them to be an issue. If you already have leaf guards, great—mention that in your Features List (see page 64). For now, what's important is that your gutters are in good working condition and clean on the outside.

Walls

The exterior paint job (if your home is painted) is the skin of your home and has a powerful impact. Warm, neutral earth tones appeal to the broadest range of potential buyers. Painting the exterior of your home is expensive, I know, but do it if you possibly can. If you can't, a good pressure washing should improve things. Be careful to adjust the pressure so it will not damage the paint. If your home is not painted, do whatever you can do to make the exterior look clean and well maintained.

Window Frames

Make sure window frame paint is in excellent condition, not cracked and peeling. Window frames can be any color that complements the home color and is in keeping with the aesthetic of the area. For instance, in the Southwest, window frames are often turquoise, which is traditionally a color believed to keep evil spirits away. If you live in Puerto Rico, Southern California, South Florida, or Hawaii, tropical colors may be appropriate. A bohemian neighborhood may also be more colorful—but aim for the middle of the range, nothing too extreme. If you're not confident with color, contact a local designer to advise you or look at the sample colors on our website.

Driveway and Walkways

The driveway and walkways greet people with either a bright smile or a tired, worn-down frown. Make them as welcoming and beautiful as possible.

Patio, Porch, Deck

These are the places where a potential buyer expects to spend leisure time, recharging, and enjoying being at home. Make sure these outside spaces are clean and well maintained, with attractive, comfortable furniture, as well as plants and flowers where appropriate. If a potential buyer feels happy at the thought of spending time on your patio, porch, or deck, that's a strong check in the YES column.

Lawn

The greener and healthier the grass, the more attractive your property will be to a buyer. If you know a year in advance that you'll be selling your home, start reseeding bare spots and getting rid of weeds. If you don't have that much lead time, do your best to make the lawn look like you care.

Hedges, Shrubs, Trees

If you have become a little relaxed about your landscaping, now is the time to give it some love. Prune trees, trim hedges and shrubs, and remove or replace any sad-looking plants so that the living things around your house look healthy and happy. Be sure to mulch!

Every penny you invest in making your landscaping beautiful will come back to you—and more—in the price you get for your home. If money is tight, sweat equity will do the job. Your hard work here is money in your pocket.

Your Home Interior

Walls

If there are cracks or holes in the walls, patch, sand, and paint them. If wallpaper is peeling, re-glue it or remove it and paint the room. If drywall tape is coming loose, smooth some drywall mud over it, let it dry, sand it, and paint it.

Choosing Colors That Sell Homes

Taste is a very individual thing. We all like different music, different foods, different colors. Some colors pull us in, while other colors turn us off. When you're selling your home, you want paint colors that appeal to the greatest number of people—and, if possible, don't turn anyone off. It's true that you will never please everyone, but if the colors of your home appeal to 80% or more of the people who come to view it, you're doing as well as you can.

Architectural styles and the colors that adorn them differ according to location and over time. Some colors can look old-fashioned. Don't be deceived by paint company brochures touting "This Year's Most Popular Colors." I recently saw a major paint company promoting an unusual shade of green as their most popular color. Decades of experience have taught me that green and yellow walls turn off many more people than they turn on.

The most pleasing and non-offensive colors are earth tones. These satisfy the largest section of the population, work for almost any architectural style, and endure. Warm earth tones have a brown foundation, while cool earth tones have a gray foundation. The colors themselves range from very light to deep. Stay with lighter colors for both interior and exterior, as lighter shades make a room feel brighter and larger.

Some people love white. Yes, white can be elegant and beautiful. But white can also feel sterile. I recently showed a 7000-square-foot home priced just under $4 million. The floors were natural wood with soft grays and shades of browns; the fireplaces were stone, and the walls were white throughout. My client loved the layout and design of this home, but something was stopping them from feeling comfortable in it. Sensing this inner conflict, I asked how they would feel if they painted the home a light gray, picking up the colors of the wood floor and the stonework. That imaginative leap immediately shifted how they felt about the home, and they made an offer on it.

Using light, neutral colors allows people to envision their own furniture and artwork in these rooms. Using strong colors reduces your pool of potential buyers, because fewer people can imagine living with them. There are exceptions, however. If your home is in the Florida Keys, the Caribbean coast of Costa Rica, or Santa Fe, New Mexico—or anywhere else with a distinct and colorful local architectural style—these suggestions may not apply to you.

Floors

Be sure all carpets look and smell clean. Rent a carpet cleaner or hire a professional to do the job. If there's a stain that won't come out, either replace the carpet or hide the stain with a throw rug.

What's under the carpet? Most houses that were built in the first thirty years of the last century have hardwood floors. Pull up a corner of the carpet and check. If there is a hardwood floor, it might be worth the effort to pull up the carpet, remove the staples, sand the wood, and varnish it. You may add a few thousand dollars to your sale price because most buyers love those beautiful original wooden floors.

Refinishing a hardwood floor may not be as expensive as you think. Pulling up carpet is just a matter of time and energy. If, because of physical or other limitations, you are not in a position to do it yourself, hire a teenager to spend a Saturday afternoon helping you. If the floor requires extensive work, like sanding and varnishing, call in a professional.

Windows

Clean, clear windows give a strong positive impression. Clean windows establish that a home is being cared for. In fact, what people notice is not clean windows, but windows that aren't clean. People want to see clearly through windows. It costs nothing but a little time and effort to clean the glass, inside and out. Do your best to replace any panes that are cracked, cloudy, or scratched. Be sure to get rid of any cobwebs between glass and screen, and wipe down the sills.

Make sure that curtains, blinds, or other window treatments are clean and functioning properly. Use curtains or shades to hide anything unsightly outside a window, such as a parking lot or a blank wall. Open them to show off a beautiful feature or view, such as a lake, a lovely old tree, or the neighbor's gorgeous garden.

Kitchen

Kitchens sell homes!

For many people, the kitchen is the most important room. It should be sparkling clean, and it should smell good. Clean your stove thoroughly. Clean the refrigerator, inside and out. Clean inside the cabinets, especially under the sink; if the bottom is permanently stained, install lining paper. If your appliances have seen better days, it is worth the investment to replace them with new ones. Dirty appliances give a bad impression; they suggest that a home is not cared for.

Bad smells turn buyers off big time. *Always* empty your trash container before a showing. If your kitchen has that stale-kitchen smell, or if the refrigerator smells bad, you're anchoring a negative in a potential buyer's mind. Don't just clean the appliances; pull them out and clean behind and under them. Odors get trapped there.

Bathrooms

Bathrooms have to be clean, and they have to smell good—but not with Febreze! It takes some time and effort, but this is something you must do. You don't want people to walk in and smell something odd, or an offensive odor emanating from the toilet seat or the floor. Clean the toilet inside and out, as well as the floor alongside and behind it. Ideally, use natural cleaning solutions with a lavender or mint scent.

Make sure there's no scum or mildew in the shower or bathtub. If there's a glass shower door, it should also be sparkling clean. Use white vinegar or specialized cleaning products to remove any water stains. Get rid of your old, sad shower curtain and replace it with a transparent shower curtain liner.

Clean inside cabinets and drawers. Use lining paper to cover up stains you can't get out.

If your bathroom mats or rugs are stained or threadbare, buy new ones. It's money well spent because you can take them with you to your next home. Invest in new, good-quality, neutral-colored towels that match the rugs. White towels and rugs can brighten up a bathroom and give it a spa-like feel.

Bedrooms

If you've got scruffy old comforters on the beds, replace them with something simple, neutral, and elegant. A white comforter in a soft-colored room is beautiful.

Remove any clutter from the top of the dresser, nightstands, and other surfaces. Organize your closets. Consider packing up some clothes to make your closets look more spacious.

Furniture

You are aiming for simple, neutral, and elegant. Rooms look bigger if they're not bursting with furniture, so remove excess furniture that makes your home feel cluttered. Also, remove anything that is unattractive or worn. I understand that might be your favorite armchair, but you can live without it for a few months.

It's okay to store things in the garage. Even better, if you can, rent a storage unit and get excess furniture away from the house.

When I'm showing a property and the potential buyers seem to like it, I find a place to sit comfortably, somewhere they can appreciate the spirit of the home. This might be the living room, the den, at the kitchen table, or outside on the deck or in the garden. I invite them to settle in, without any need to hurry off, and begin a conversation about things other than the property. We talk about their kids, places they've been, places they like. This allows them to experience being in the home in more normal circumstances. Eventually, I may remark, "This is such a comfortable room, isn't it?" If the potential buyers realize that yes, they do feel comfortable in this home, they are far more likely to make an offer.

Not every buyer's broker will do this. But if your couch and chairs are comfortable, you are doing what you can to make it happen.

If there are fixtures in your home that you plan to take with you, such as chandeliers, wall sconces, mounted mirrors, curtains or blinds, or garden fountains and sculptures, it is best to remove them before putting your home on the market and replace them with something neutral and appealing. If you don't do this, a buyer may become attached to an item and it can become a sticking point in the negotiation.

Photos and Personal Items

Most real estate agents tell sellers to remove *all* personal photos. Once again, I don't agree. You want your home to feel like a home, and photos of your loved ones contribute to that. But I have been in homes where personal photos crowd every available surface. This will not help you achieve a sale.

A few personal items make a home seem warm, comfortable, lived-in. Too many makes it psychologically difficult for potential buyers to imagine themselves living there.

I also recommend that you pack up all religious items. As a spiritual person, you carry your relationship with God or a higher power within you, so ask yourself if you can do without the physical items or images for a short time. Also, remove any political items. Many people have powerful ideas about religion and politics, and may react negatively if their views or beliefs differ from yours.

Lighting

Always turn on all lights before a showing, even end table lamps. Even on a sunny day, a home looks more inviting with the lights on.

Lighting is critically important in showcasing a living space. Good lighting can transform a room from dull and average into a beautiful, elegant, almost magical place. If you haven't yet delved into lighting design, now is the time to focus on that integral component of your interior décor.

Ceiling Lights

If you have recessed lighting in the ceiling, change out flood-light bulbs for dimmable halogen spotlights. Use PAR20 or 30, depending on the size of your cans, and 50W or 75W depending on how bright you want them to be. The results will be lighting similar to what you'd find in a high-end art gallery. These bulbs are not energy efficient, but the effect in creating atmosphere is remarkable.

A few years ago, a client listed a home with me for $2 million. In total, there were 240 can lights throughout the home, all fitted with floodlight bulbs which produced an ugly washed-out light. I recommended that he change out all the bulbs to dimmable, PAR30, 75W halogen spots, at a cost of about $9 each. Reluctantly, he agreed to this considerable expense, and requested that if the new bulbs did not make the remarkable change I assured him they would, I would pay for the bulbs. I agreed. The transformation was truly spectacular, and when he saw it he was blown away.

If you do not have dimmer switches, install them everywhere. Dimmers allow you to set the atmosphere to the exact lighting you want for any experience, and for any time of day or night. I ask all of my seller clients to do this immediately if it is financially possible.

Lighting Fixtures

Sometimes the most discreet things leave the greatest impression, and lighting fixtures are one of those things. Good lighting fixtures sell homes! Invest in beautiful lighting fixtures that complement the style of your home: chandeliers, floor lamps, and table lamps. If you don't trust your own judgment, ask an interior decorator for advice. If you let the decorator purchase the light fixtures, you will pay a premium price, so you'll save money if you ask for photos of what they recommend and then find similar fixtures yourself.

Exterior and Landscape Lighting

This is especially important if your home will be on the market when potential buyers may arrive to view it in the dark. Thoughtfully placed exterior lighting gives the impression that this is a high-quality property, owned by someone with taste. It sets an expectation, before the buyer even walks in the door, that they will be impressed by your home.

Landscape lighting transforms a regular yard into a place of elegance and beauty, and need not be expensive: some solar lights cost less than ten dollars apiece.

Staging

If you have to move before your home sells, you have a fresh challenge. You have two choices: leave your property empty and clean, or stage it. Staging means dressing the property with furniture, art, and knick-knacks to give the appearance that it is lived in. Don't make the mistake of assuming that potential buyers can imagine what an empty room will feel like with their belongings in it. Almost always, they can't.

Imagine walking into a house you are thinking about buying and seeing empty, cavernous rooms, with no warmth and no light other than a bare bulb hanging from the ceiling. Now imagine yourself walking into a home that is tastefully, simply appointed, with lamps shedding a warm glow. Furnishings and décor stir the imagination of potential buyers. They turn a building into a home. Remember that buyers rarely make the effort to imagine what could be, if there's nothing in front of their eyes to prompt them.

Staging is important, so do it if you can. Paint the walls and clean the carpets. Leave a few pieces of neutral, handpicked artwork on the walls. If you can live with a little less furniture for a while and the moving distance isn't an obstacle, leave a nice couch, coffee table, and chair in the living room. Leave a bed, a dresser, even a rug—as long as it's a nice, clean rug—in a bedroom.

The amount of staging can vary, from a few well-placed pieces of furniture that suggest how a room can be used to a full semblance of family life, including books on the bookshelves, a computer on the desk, a television, towels in the bathroom, family photographs and ornaments, etc. Anything that brings life into a vacant property is a good thing.

When you stage a room, look back at it as you walk out and ask yourself, "Is it simple, neutral, and elegant?" For example, don't use gaudy or overly rustic furniture. It's better to have potential buyers say nothing about the furniture than have them say, "That's awful." We don't want them to admire the furniture, either. We want them to walk in and say, "What a beautiful room, what a beautiful house." The furniture they're seeing should be inconsequential.

Appeal to the Buyer's Senses

When people arrive to view your home, they have an immediate sensory experience—before they're even aware of it. It may be delightful, making them want to come back again, and maybe making them want this to be their home. Or it may be negative, turning them off the property before they've even really seen it.

So, be aware of the sounds that potential buyers will hear. The smells they'll smell. And of course, as I detailed earlier, the things they'll see—or not see.

Pleasant Sounds Or Unpleasant Noises

You want to create a pleasant environment. You may think, "I'll have my favorite Beethoven symphony playing when they come." That might be the potential buyer's favorite music, too—but what if they hate classical music? What if that symphony triggers a terrible memory? It's risky to have music playing when your house is being shown. Do this only if you are trying to cover up annoying sounds in the neighborhood—and only if those annoying sounds really are covered up. If you decide to play music, a light New Age station or soft Spanish guitar are probably the most universally non-offensive styles of music.

Smells

Some people put cookies or bread in to bake when potential buyers come to view a property. It's a great idea—who doesn't like the smell of freshly baked cookies? Hot mulled apple cider also fills a house with wonderful aromas. Some people brew coffee, but I don't recommend it, because it makes your home smell like a coffee shop.

The only smells you want are delicious aromas from the kitchen or the fragrance of fresh flowers arranged in a vase. Avoid perfume, incense, room fresheners, and diffusers. Many people are sensitive or allergic to scented products, and since these are often used to cover up unpleasant smells, they create suspicion in the mind of a potential buyer. If you must use a room scent, choose something natural like lavender or mint. Some high-quality wall diffusers such as those from Scentsy provide subtle natural and non-chemical aromas than can work.

Ozonators are good at removing unpleasant smells, but if you don't get at the source of the smell, it will come back. A foul smell is being caused by something. Find out what it is and get rid of it.

One of the most difficult smells to deal with is mildew. The only way to get rid of the smell is to get rid of the mildew, which may be expensive. If you have mildew or mold, there is a humidity problem—maybe a leak or some other cause of moisture that is encouraging the mildew to grow. This is a serious problem. It is probably affecting your health, and it is also a disclosure issue (see page 81). If you have mold or mildew, deal with it now.

Pets

The smell of animals is a big negative check mark for most buyers and can be devastating to a sale. I strongly recommend you move your pets out of the house while it's on the market. If that isn't possible, make sure the cat litter box is clean and discreetly placed (ideally, in the garage or utility room). Bathe dogs once a week or more with a lightly scented shampoo. If your pet has left stains anywhere in the house, scrub the area well and make sure it doesn't happen again.

Many people are allergic to cats, and it is almost impossible to keep a house free of cat dander, which is the allergen. I had one client leave a house after five minutes, saying, "If we had been in there any longer, I wouldn't have been able to breathe." If you have a cat, vacuum thoroughly, not just the floors but all furniture, too, even if you've found a temporary home for your furry friend. If the cat is still in residence, you must do this before every showing, and disclose the presence of a cat to the buyer's broker whenever a showing is scheduled.

CHAPTER 7

Marketing Strategy and Materials

Presenting your house to the public is the responsibility of your broker, but it's up to you to make sure they're doing a good job. Don't be afraid to make suggestions or request that something be redone if you feel it's not quite right or could be done better.

When to List Your Home

Selling real estate is a numbers game. The more people who walk through the door, the higher the likelihood of a sale—and the better job you do at marketing your home, the more people will come to see it. If fifty potential buyers come to view your home, you have a much greater chance of selling it than if you only get ten.

Most real estate brokers will recommend that you list your home early in the high traffic season for your area. In many places, you hear that winter is slow and sales pick up in the spring, so they'll suggest that you wait until early spring to list your home. I don't agree. I recommend sellers put their home on the market when they are ready to sell it. Don't wait! You never know when that buyer who is looking for your exact property will be in your town looking to buy.

Because of the widespread practice of delaying the listing of a property, the off-season is when the fewest number of homes are on the market. Fewer homes on the market means less competition for you. I've lost count of how many times I have had to convince sellers to keep their homes on the market in the winter, or to go ahead and list their homes in the off-season, and they sell. Yes, in the off-season! And usually at a great price, too, because there is very little competition.

The only negative about listing in the winter is the photography of the exterior of your home and garden—unless your home is in a winter sports destination, in which case winter is high season. So, if your home has not sold by spring, have the photographer return once things look green and gorgeous and re-photograph the exterior, and possibly include some interior shots that show the view or the garden through a window.

People buy homes they fall in love with. Excellent marketing presents your property in a way that makes potential buyers excited to see it. Your home should be represented honestly and beautifully. I say "honestly," because there's no point in misleading other brokers and potential buyers. If the marketing materials promise something that isn't really true, brokers and buyers will only be disappointed when they see the property in person, and angry that you and your broker have wasted their time.

It is your real estate broker's job to create marketing materials directed toward other brokers and their clients, as well as materials for the public. Realistically, the lower the price of a property, the smaller the commission, and therefore the less money your broker may be able or willing to spend on marketing. This is especially true if they believe that, for whatever reason, your property may be difficult to sell.

If your broker is unwilling to cover the costs of creating the marketing materials you want and deserve (photography, brochures, virtual tour, website, etc.), and you are happy with your choice of broker in every other respect, you may decide to contribute to the marketing expenses. If you do this, request to be repaid out of the commission when the property sells. Be sure to include this point in your listing contract or marketing addendum.

Main Photo

When you look at property listings online, what's the first thing that catches your eye? The main photo. If the photo grabs you, you'll click through to learn more about the property, or, if you're looking at a real estate magazine, you may make a note to follow up with a real estate agent. And if that photo doesn't grab you? You will just keep scrolling or turning the pages.

If you like fishing, think of the difference between an enticing photo and a repulsive photo as the difference between baiting your hook with a big live shrimp or an old dried-up one. The fish are going to head straight for that big live shrimp, and they'll swim right past the old dried-up one. You only have a moment to hook a buyer into wanting to see your home or an agent into wanting to show your home. Bait that hook well!

Don't let your agent skimp on photography. Insist on an experienced real estate photographer, no matter the price of your home. A professional photo shoot can range from $100 to $5,000, depending on the property, the area, and the skills and services offered by the photographer. A Photography Preparation Checklist is available at HowToSellYourHomeNow.us.

Most MLS's require that the main photo be of the exterior, and the online format requires it to be oriented horizontally ("landscape" mode). Instruct your broker to request several photos of the exterior from different perspectives, and review them with your broker. Choose the photo that would make *you* want to see your home if you were looking to buy. If your home has a magnificent view, make sure your cover photo shows the view. I know that can be difficult to achieve, but it is very important: views sell homes!

A great cover photo intrigues potential buyers, even if your home may not be exactly the sort of property they're looking for.

Additional Photography

You can catch a buyer's attention with an inspiring, compelling main photo, but as they click through your listing, photo by photo, it's vital that the images continue to hold their attention. This is why professional photography is essential in marketing. As I mentioned earlier, your photography must inspire the viewer—and it must also be honest. Some photographers use wide-angle lenses that exaggerate the size of rooms far too much. Sure, those photos will pull in buyers, but you don't want a buyer to walk in the door and immediately feel that the photos misrepresented the size of the rooms. A disappointed buyer is not what you want. A good photographer can capture beautiful photos of your home without such exaggeration. You don't need photos of everything, either: skip closets (unless they are amazing), most bathrooms, storage closets, and the garage (unless it is amazing). If your home has views, be sure to require photos showing the view from different rooms, as well as from the deck or terrace. Also, if you have a nice yard or landscaping, make sure that is among your photographs. Beautiful yards and landscaping excite and inspire.

Title

The fantastic main photo caught their attention. The title gets them through the door. On printed marketing materials, the viewer will see the photo and almost simultaneously read the title. Think of it like an invitation to a party that you don't want this potential buyer to miss.

People who are looking for a new home are looking for a connection. They want to fall in love with the vision of themselves in this home. Titles that capture this romantic ideal are the titles that will get them to say, "I have to see this place."

So don't limit your title to mere information. Be creative—and encourage your broker to be creative. Use adjectives. Don't be afraid to step outside the box.

What if you were looking for a new home and saw the title "Mesmerizing Home on Beaver Lake." You'd want to find out what's so mesmerizing about it. Immediately you're more interested in seeing this home than you are in seeing "Large Home on Beaver Lake." Nothing enticing there, unless Beaver Lake is the only place you want to be.

Description

You've grabbed their attention with a spectacular photo and excited their imagination with a seductive title. If they're browsing online, they've clicked through to the full description. If they're sitting in a broker's office, they've decided to read your listing rather than moving on to the next one. If they like what they see, the next step is scheduling an appointment to see your home in person.

Make sure your broker prepares two versions of the description: one short, for the MLS listing (the broker will know the maximum number of characters allowed by your local MLS), and a longer, two- or three-paragraph description for your brochure and property webpage or website. Let your broker know you are expecting excellence, and offer them the guidelines on the following page. If you are under-impressed by your broker's writing skills, edit or rewrite the description yourself, or insist that your broker hire a professional writer.

An effective description focuses on the aspects of your property that are the most appealing, and anything that sets it apart from similar properties. Keep it simple, but use subtle and brilliant adjectives that speak to the buyer's desire for a romantic connection with this property, which may become their home.

Many real estate agents try to include as many specific details as possible. I believe that is a mistake. Instead of peppering potential buyers with information, entice them. Appeal to their emotions and imagination. Make them want to know more about this property. They can always fill in the details later, once they have made an emotional connection with it.

The details of the property are provided on the MLS—lot size, number of bedrooms and bathrooms, etc.—so don't waste space in the description by repeating them. Dwell on the things you love about your home, the things a buyer is likely to appreciate. Use phrases that suggest the experience of living happily in this home. If the presentation moves them, they may even be prepared to compromise on any practical details that weren't what they were looking for, and come to view your home, anyway.

Be sure to include any features that make your home stand out, such as

☞ Sweeping views of the city, mountains, lake, etc.
☞ Water features such as a stream or pond
☞ Green or sustainable built home
☞ Expansive modern kitchen
☞ Breathtaking sunsets from the deck
☞ Intimate entertainment areas
☞ Luscious organic garden
☞ Vibrant perennial garden
☞ Serene and spacious master bedroom

I have seen descriptions of properties with an amazing view in which the view was not displayed in the photos and not mentioned in the description! That kind of thing shocks me. An agent who lets something like that slip by is lazy and incompetent—and should be fired.

Features List

This is where you get to share with potential buyers everything you love about your home, in elaborate detail. What would matter to you if you were the buyer?

Break the list into categories, such as Home Exterior Features, Interior Features, Construction, Kitchen, Living Areas, Electronics, etc. Don't feel that you have to stick to these categories; you can organize the list in whatever way makes the most sense for your home. Some kitchens may have 20 desirable features, where others may have only a few. The idea is to highlight the parts of your home where there are important features to note.

You need to do this task yourself. Your real estate broker can help, but you are the one who knows your home. Mention how much you love the sound of birds singing above your rear deck, or the amazing views from the master bedroom. Dig deep and don't hold back!

Property Details

Carefully review all the details that will be provided on the MLS and other marketing materials before they're published. Check for all possible errors. Perhaps the dimensions of a room are wrong. Perhaps there's a room that's not being used as a bedroom but could be, if you added a closet. That bonus room your broker omitted might be what makes the difference for a buyer.

IMPORTANT: Make sure the square footage in your listing is accurate. If you do not have a floor plan with the square footage, or a recent appraisal which included measurements, you will need to hire someone to create an accurate floor plan. Misrepresenting the size of your home can lead to serious negative consequences, even a lawsuit. Make sure your real estate broker gets this right!

The number of bedrooms and bathrooms matters, but don't misrepresent them. Be clear that that potential extra bedroom lacks a closet. Potential buyers will discover the truth when they view your home, and nobody likes to feel they've been misled.

If you find a mistake, no matter how small, contact your broker immediately. It's not a question of blame—it's a question of accuracy. Your broker should be grateful that you've spotted the correction in time.

Property Website

Some real estate companies create a dedicated website for your property as part of their service. This allows buyers to take an experiential journey through your home and the community it belongs to. It gives potential buyers the fullest possible idea of what it would be like to live in your home. The more information you can provide, the better.

The homepage should have an interesting title and cover photo. If it's different from the one on the MLS and brochure, that's even better. "Oh, wow," is the reaction you're aiming for. Follow this up with an enticing description. Make it more informative than anything that appears elsewhere, but keep it succinct.

People don't like to read huge chunks of text. Remember to use words that conjure up the experience a potential buyer would have if your home was theirs.

The website should include a photo gallery. The MLS often limits your photos, but a website does not. That doesn't mean you should include everything. Choose high-quality photos only, and label each one: "View from the master bedroom," "Built-in bookcase in the family room," "Doorway between the great room and the enclosed porch," etc. Since space is virtually unlimited, show the street, the houses next door, and any nearby amenities such as a park or lakefront or ski area. If there is a railroad track or some other drawback, let people see it: make it an asset if you can rather than ignoring it. For example, romanticize the experience of living in a home where you hear the whistle of a train going by. You don't want buyers to have any unpleasant surprises when they see or hear these things for themselves.

Charm people with places of interest in the area that make you happy: a cool little coffee shop, a well-stocked bookstore, the plaza where local events take place. Or a cinema, a theater, a skateboard park: whatever makes your neighborhood special. You might even include photos of nearby spots for weekend getaways, and a separate page for nearby towns. Include links to the websites of entertainment venues, so people can take an experiential journey through the community to help cement their attraction.

Include a map plug-in, which will give visitors an aerial view and also let them come down to street level and get a sense of the surroundings. Most map apps provide a widget that shows the exact location of your home.

Add a footer on every page giving your broker's name and phone number, so buyers who don't have their own broker will have someone to call. Your real estate agent should also create a separate non-branded website.

The address of your property is a good domain name. If 9meadowbrookdrive.com isn't available, try MeadowbrookHome.com or 9Meadowbrook.com. The URL should appear clearly on all promotional materials. For the non-branded URL, change the name slightly, maybe by adding or removing the word "road."

Do not overlook this important marketing tool. It will increase the number of buyers who decide to visit your home and experience it for themselves. If your broker's agency does not offer this service, consider creating a website yourself or hiring someone to do it for you.

Virtual Tour

Virtual tours come in many forms. Some brokers make a video of the home and use that as a virtual tour. The newest technology, called Matterport, provides a 3-D tour that the viewer can direct, as if they are virtually walking through the home. I have two problems with this technology. First, though the tour is realistic, it feels distorted. Second, when a potential buyer tours your home with this technology, they will decide yes or no right then and there, without ever seeing your home in person and accurately experiencing its spirit. My preference is simply a slide show of your best photographs set to music. A higher-level slide show can be created in iMovie (Mac or iPad) or Movie Maker (Windows) using the "Ken Burns" effect, which makes a still photo look like it's moving by creating elegant pan and zoom transitions between images. This is a beautiful, low-cost way to simulate a video.

Materials for Buyers

When buyers visit a property, they should leave with printed material that will remind them of its best features. Many agents produce a booklet, up to 20 pages long, which includes lots of photos and lists all the details and all the upgrades of the property, along with a floor plan. I think this is unnecessary. You don't want to overwhelm a buyer with too much information. You want them to leave with just enough so they retain a taste of what they saw in your home, and enough to inspire them to want to return and learn more. I prefer a buyer ask questions or request the floor plan rather than handing it all to them up

Mishaps Occur

An Interesting Mistake

I was once selling a home with a spectacular view of the city of Asheville, NC. The photo we took was iconic, so I created 18" x 70" posters of it and gave one to each potential buyer, wanting to capitalize on the property's huge selling point: the magnificent view of downtown. After 20 showings and giving away 20+ posters, it hit me that I was letting the buyers leave with the amazing view in their hand, rather than with a memory of the view which they would want to come back and see in person again.

front. I want them to be engaged and wanting more. That's what will keep them thinking about your home.

You did your best to make the experience of walking through your home amazing. Hopefully, these potential buyers are feeling intrigued by its potential as their home. Now, give them just enough information to take away so they won't forget why they liked it—but not so much that they feel like the experience is complete. If the brochure leaves them, ever so slightly, wanting more, they're more likely to come back for a second viewing.

Simple and elegant is always better. A well-designed, professionally produced, four-page brochure, printed on a 17" x 11" heavier stock paper and folded in half, is all you need. It can be printed quickly and affordably, then left in the home for visiting buyers and mailed out to other brokers and buyers considering whether to view the property in person. The front should feature that enticing title and your favorite cover photo (interior or exterior). Inside, smaller photos of your home's best features accompany the description.

A cheaper option, for lower-priced properties, is a single 8½" x 11" sheet printed on semi-gloss card stock, with color photos on the front and information on the back. These could cost as little as a dollar apiece.

Consider creating a list of utility costs over the past year, month by month. This might include electricity, gas, propane, water, garbage collection, and yard work, along with property taxes and any Home Owners Association or condominium costs. Buyers appreciate this.

Branded and Unbranded Marketing Materials

When creating your home's marketing materials, your real estate agent should create two versions of each: one branded and the other unbranded. Branded simply means that the material has the broker's company logo, along with (sometimes) the broker's photo, and their contact information. Unbranded means that the material has no listing-agent information on it.

The reason for this is so that other brokers can give their clients the unbranded version and add their own information. Reasonably, they want to protect their relationship with their client. It's not unheard of for a buyer to go around their broker, who has introduced them to the property, and contact the seller's broker directly, in the hope of saving money by working directly with the listing broker and negotiating the commission down. This is an ugly move for a buyer to make and usually does not achieve the desired goal, instead creating a cloud of bad will all around.

Broker-to-Broker Marketing

Once your home has been accurately priced, a marketing strategy decided upon, and marketing materials produced, your broker should send out an email blast introducing your home to all the brokers in your area. This is basically an electronic brochure: a one-page piece with a title, a few photos, the address, and the MLS number, along with links to the MLS listing, your property's website, and the video tour.

Another excellent broker-to-broker marketing tool is a 5" x 7" postcard. On one side is the cover photo and title, with an inset photo of the kitchen or some other feature that will make a buyer say, "Wow." On the back is the address of the property, a brief description or just a list of the seven most important details along with the URL of the unbranded website containing full details. On the right-hand side is a blank space so the postcard can be addressed and mailed out. Your broker can send these postcards to other brokers and clients, and leave a stack in the property for other brokers to take so they can do the same, adding a note that goes something like, "Saw this home and thought of you! If it looks appealing, check it out online and call me if you're interested."

CHAPTER 8

Showing Your Home

It's a good idea to leave your home when it is being shown. Your presence can make potential buyers feel pressured and uncomfortable speaking honestly with their broker about the property, and it makes it harder for them to imagine themselves living in the home if the current occupant is there.

After every showing to a buyer, your real estate broker should receive feedback from the buyer's broker within a day or so. This is where you will learn what it was about your home that did not work for that potential buyer—or whether you might receive an offer before long. Don't take negative comments personally! This is valuable information. Look for recurring themes, and if possible address any issues that come up repeatedly.

Some things you can't fix, such as highway noise. Here are a few examples of things that can be fixed:

☞ If three potential buyers in a row say your property is overpriced, adjust the price.

☞ If even one potential buyer complains about a smell in the basement, hunt it down and eliminate it. Mold and mildew discovered in a home will kill a sale. Hire a mold/mildew professional to fix the problem.

☞ If a potential buyer says the house is too dark, turn on more lights, add more lamps, or open the curtains and/or blinds.

☞ If a potential buyer complains about the smell of your pet, either increase the frequency of grooming or find a temporary home for your pet until you sell your home.

☞ If a potential buyer complains the house feels cold, assess whether this is a temperature issue or a décor issue. Turn up the thermostat, use warmer lightbulbs, or add some colorful throw pillows.

Try not to feel frustrated when you get stupid comments. I once read a criticism of a property for having too many stairs, when the description said it's a three-story house! Or you might get the criticism that your home is too far out of town, when your description says it's 20 minutes from town and the map app shows its exact location.

Frustration is just part of the process. A buyer's broker may sometimes not even turn up for an appointment, and just call to say that they drove by and the client did not like the location, or that they ran out of time—and that's after you spent hours getting your home show-ready for this appointment. As inconsiderate as this is, it happens. As a buyer's broker, I try never to let this happen. When I make an appointment with a seller, I show up, even if the buyer wants to blow it off. I explain that the seller has spent valuable time preparing their home for the viewing, and it would be discourteous not to stop by briefly, at least—and I have never had a buyer refuse to be courteous. Unfortunately, not all real estate agents have this awareness.

Open Houses

The value of an open house varies according to where you live. In some markets, an open house is *the* way to launch a new property on the market, and the turnout is almost always impressive. In other markets, an open house can feel like a waste of time and money, because often very few people show up other than neighbors curious to see the inside of your home. Let your agent be your guide. If open houses work in your market, your real estate broker will want to have one immediately after your listing goes live. Usually the broker covers the cost of any food and beverages offered. The seller may want to contribute fresh flowers, and take the food and beverages up a notch. If your home is priced at a million dollars or more, you might serve some special tapas, caviar, or sushi, and offer an appropriate wine or champagne.

There are three different types of open houses:

Public Open House

A public open house gives potential buyers an opportunity to walk through your home without a real estate agent accompanying them, so they can see how it feels. Such open houses are promoted to the public via local media and real estate websites. They are usually held on weekends, when people are less likely to be at their jobs. It is common to put up signs saying "Open House" and offer at least a beverage to visitors, along with a brochure, a copy of the MLS listing, and a Features List.

Broker Open House

A broker open house introduces your home to the real estate brokers in your market and is promoted directly to your community's real estate professionals. It gives agents a chance to preview your home, and often a chance to connect with colleagues over food and drinks. The best time is a weekday lunchtime. Make sure you have a delicious menu and interesting beverages—this can influence some brokers' decisions regarding which open house to attend. Another good time for a broker open house is Friday late afternoon, at the end of the work week, with cocktails and delicious hors d'oeuvres.

Make sure broker open houses include survey cards. These provide you and your broker feedback from the professionals who will bring potential buyers to your home. Keep the cards anonymous—you want those who attend to feel able to share their honest thoughts about your home and your asking price.

Broker/Public Open House

This open house covers it all and is promoted to everyone. It's best to hold this open house on a weekend afternoon. Go big, with great food and beverages. If you have the space, you might even have a string quartet or a classical guitarist.

Security

Open houses create opportunities for things to go missing. Be sure to lock all valuables safely away, such as jewelry or table-top artworks—anything that can fit in a pocket or handbag. Depending on the size of your home and the turnout your real estate agent expects, you might ask your broker to arrange for personnel from their firm to be present, to keep a watchful eye on the traffic.

Congratulations! All your hard work has paid off, and you've received an offer—maybe more than one. Now what?

Part Three

THE SALE

CHAPTER 9

Negotiating with the Buyer

Your broker has called with the good news. Hopefully, the offer is for the full asking price or close to it. In the right market, this is certainly possible. Chances are, however, that the first offer you receive will be lower than what you're asking—maybe much lower. Don't get upset. This is not a reflection on your home. If you view a low offer as disrespectful or insulting, that's a sign that you are operating from your emotional brain, not your rational brain.

As the seller, you are undergoing a doubly emotional experience. First, you're selling your home. You've put a great deal of work, creativity, money, and time into it. You've had happy times and sad times in it. Perhaps you've raised your family in it. You're proud of every thoughtful touch, and you want it to be appreciated. Second, you're hoping to bring in a good amount of money—which, in most cases, has been borrowed against in the form of a mortgage. If you don't find a buyer—and at the price you're hoping for—you may face unpleasant financial consequences. Even if a mortgage is not an issue, future plans will usually hinge on this sale.

For a seller, often both financial security and emotional security are at stake.

Conversely, a buyer has no deep emotional attachment to this property. It holds promise for the future—they can and even want to imagine themselves living in it—but they can walk away. Think of buyers as having one overriding goal: to get the best deal possible. They are operating strategically. They are unlikely to say, "Oh, this is exactly what we've been dreaming about! George, come look at this gorgeous kitchen!" They will usually be as unenthusiastic as they can manage as they tour your home. They won't normally congratulate you, or even comment, on your thoughtful touches. They may be critical, even of things that don't deserve criticism. You may get a long list of everything "wrong" with your home. The last thing a buyer wants is for you to think they love your property so much that they'll pay a premium for it. There is the rare exception, but it is extremely rare.

Your broker, who also has no emotional investment in your home, is better able to make objective judgments and advise you accordingly. A good real estate agent will be patient and understand your emotional investment, softening the impact of a low offer by saying something like, "This is not a great offer, but it is an offer. You get to decide whether or not to accept it."

If the offer has the potential to meet your requirements, your agent will encourage you to negotiate. What is the best counter-offer to make at this point? Are there other factors that might make a difference to this buyer? An experienced real estate broker will know how to respond in a way that helps the buyer see the value in your home, and how to counter the usual tactics of the buyer's agent.

There are three simple rules in negotiating. Following them ensures you will get the best price for your home *from this buyer.*

Rule #1: Don't Take It Personally.

I know. This is your home, and you have a lot invested in it. But it won't be your home for much longer. It's probably your biggest asset, and that's how you need to think of it—as an asset that you're liquidating. You may even be selling it at a loss, which will make the negotiation harder. Allowing your emotions free rein will make the process unnecessarily difficult. You may need to do a lot of deep breathing and releasing, letting go... (For more on letting go of your home, see page 107 and following.)

Rule #2: Know Your Lowest Acceptable Price—Before You Begin.

Set a bar that you will not go below, no matter what. If, after negotiations, the buyer offers one penny less than your predetermined threshold amount, you walk away. Knowing this will give you a sense of strength and calm.

Rule #3: Take Your Time.

An offer usually comes with a deadline, at which time it will expire. Don't rush to respond. Take your time to think the offer over. Give it 24 hours, at least. You don't want to appear anxious or desperate to sell. The signal you want to send is that you are not in any hurry. Even if you are!

There are also three simple moves in negotiating.

Negotiate. Make Three Moves: Your First, Your Second, and Your Final One.

Move 1. Let's say you've received an offer 30% under your asking price, and your lowest acceptable price is 15% under your asking price. Counter the offer with a 5% reduction in your asking price.

Move 2. The buyer raises the offer to 25% below your asking price, you drop your price by another 5%, taking you to 10% below your asking price.

Move 3. Wait for the buyer's next counter—though with luck they will accept your previous counter. If not, make this your last price reduction. Drop your price to 15% below the asking price—your lowest acceptable price—and let the buyer know that this is your final offer.

No matter how low the initial offer, do not reject it out of hand. Don't take it personally. I have had offers come in for less than half of the asking price, and when the negotiation was over, the buyer agreed to pay just 10% under the asking price. Buyers will often test the water to see how far down you'll go.

Stay at the negotiating table. Make your three moves, maybe even four—and then walk away if the buyer will not agree to your lowest acceptable price. Trust that another buyer will appear. Sometimes, after you have ended a negotiation, the buyer will return a few days later with a more reasonable offer.

And don't assume that whatever the offer is, another buyer will offer more. It's not uncommon for the first offer to be the highest and best you receive.

Furniture

Including furnishings in the sale price of your home is a bad idea. Don't do it, unless you are selling a rental home that is being purchased as an investment property. If you include furniture in the sale price, what do you think the buyer will do if they don't want it? They'll put a (probably too high) value on the furniture and try to negotiate the price down accordingly. Things will get messy and confused very quickly.

The exception to this would be if your home is in a vacation destination and the buyer will likely use it part-time and rent it out to tourists when they're not using it.

If you are open to selling all or some of your furniture, you can always let the buyer's broker know that. Clarify that the sale of any furniture will be discussed only after you come to terms on the sale of the house—after the negotiation has been completed and the property is under contract. Create a separate bill of sale for the furniture. You should not be expected to pay either your broker or the buyer's broker a fee or commission on the sale of personal property.

CHAPTER 10

Inspections, Disclosures, Appraisals

Inspections and Disclosures

Once you accept an offer, the buyer will arrange for a licensed home inspector to inspect the home. Mortgage lenders demand an inspection, and even a cash buyer would be foolish to buy a home without ensuring that any problems are brought to light.

In most states, you and your real estate agent are legally required to disclose "material facts" about your home. As I mentioned on page 33, some states allow you to make "No representation"–though your agent is still obliged to inform the buyer of any material facts of which they have knowledge. "Material facts" refers to any information about a property that would affect a buyer's decision to purchase it, or affect the buyer's perceived value of a property.

Material Facts

In real estate, a material fact is information that, if known, might cause a buyer to make a different decision about remaining in a purchase contract, or about the price paid or received for a property.

Once again, I encourage you to be honest and forthright. If problems with the property are discovered in the inspection phase, the buyer will almost certainly request that the issues be repaired or that the purchase price be reduced to cover those repairs. And if a buyer feels that you deliberately concealed problems, you will lose their trust and will probably lose the sale.

It's a good idea to have your home inspected before you put it on the market. Doing so will alert you to any issues that might show up in a buyer's inspection. Fix the problems if you can; otherwise, if a major issue comes to light at the negotiating stage, it may cost you a great deal of money. Provide your agent with a copy of the inspection report, and have them attach it to the listing along with a statement of the repairs that have been made. Your buyer may even choose to forgo an inspection if they feel good about yours.

If you cannot afford to have the work done, do what you can. Find out the exact scope and scale of any major problem, and get two or three companies to give you a quote for fixing it. Make sure the quote says, "We have identified the source of the issue and we can repair it for a cost of..." Require the company to guarantee that, for this price, the problem will be entirely remedied.

Tell your agent and potential buyers that the problem exists, and what it will cost to fix it. Share the quotes. If anyone asks why you don't fix the problem yourself, tell the truth, but say, "We will deduct the cost of repair from the sale price." (The quotes can be included in the sale documents.) As additional assurance to a buyer, you might even agree to leave a further amount in escrow for three months, or whatever is a reasonable time for the buyer to be satisfied that the issue has been resolved.

Appraisals

If your buyer is borrowing money to purchase your home, his bank or mortgage company will require an appraisal from a licensed professional. Even if your buyer is paying cash, they may order an appraisal to ensure that they are not overpaying for your home.

An appraisal will either solidify the sale or kill it. So be prepared. Ask your real estate agent to update the CMA (Comparative Market Analysis) if it's been a while since they first did one for you, or provide you with MLS sheets for comparable proper- ties that will support the contract price. If you have created a Features List, be sure to include that, too.

Even if the bank doesn't require it, I strongly recommend you get an appraisal of your home before placing it on the market, and list it at a price that is supported by the appraisal. If you have followed my advice, include that appraisal with the other documents mentioned earlier.

If your real estate broker knows the appraiser and has a positive relationship with them, ask them to meet the appraiser at your house and hand them the supporting information. If your agent does not know the appraiser, you can give them the information yourself, explaining that your broker prepared it to aid in determining their appraisal. Even if you have prepared a Features List, show off those features to the appraiser.

Your home should be impeccable, just as if you were preparing it for a showing. Usually, you have only one shot with an appraiser, so you want them to come up with a valuation that is as high as possible. If it comes in below the contract price, you can expect a take-it-or-leave-it situation: either you accept the appraiser's valuation as the contract price, or you lose the sale.

It's virtually impossible to dispute a low appraisal after it's done. Most appraisers will defend their valuation to the end, especially if they have been hired by a bank or mortgage company—they do not want to appear incompetent. That is why it's vital to make sure they have all the information possible to defend your sale price *before* they come up with their figure.

CHAPTER 11

Legal Documents

Every residential real estate contract contains fundamental elements that must be agreed upon, usually through negotiation. How these are structured in the contract varies from state to state.

Make sure your real estate agent explains each clause to you clearly. Don't just blindly trust and sign.

Hire a Real Estate Attorney

I strongly recommend that you use a real estate attorney. This is the norm in most areas of the U.S., and even where it isn't the norm, it's a good idea. The documents pertaining to the sale of a property are binding legal documents. A broker is not a lawyer and therefore cannot provide legal advice or draft contractual terms between buyer and seller. *Be sure you hire an attorney who specializes in or who has extensive experience in real estate transactions.*

Most real estate attorneys have a standard fee for handling a transaction on behalf of the buyer or the seller. These may vary according to the type of property and the sale price. I recommend involving your attorney as early as possible, since in most cases it will not affect the amount of money you pay them.

As a seller, you need to know:

☞ Your property deed is conveyed correctly.
☞ Your mortgage or other liens are paid off.
☞ Similarly, any taxes due are paid from the proceeds of the sale.

Attorney fees for standard residential real estate transactions will vary depending on the price, but normally range between $500 and $1,250. Ask the attorney what they will charge before you hire them. This is money well invested, as you will be assured that everything has been done correctly and the attorney carries the liability if anything is done wrong. Your interests are not opposed to the interests of the buyer, so it is possible for you both to use the same attorney, thus reducing the cost.

The Sale Contract, Or Offer to Purchase

- ❶ **Sale Price.** Be sure this is as agreed, and any owner-financing arrangements are accurate.
- ❶ **Due Diligence Period.** This is the time period you provide to the buyer for them to complete their inspections of your home and to get a final commitment from their mortgage lender. During this period buyers can rescind or terminate their offer without forfeiting any of their Earnest Money. A termination by a buyer must be formally communicated to you and your real estate broker before 5:00 p.m. or midnight on the last day of the Due Diligence period in order for them to be entitled to a full reimbursement of their Earnest Money. If a buyer decides to terminate their offer after the Due Diligence period, the rules of how the Earnest Money deposit is handled vary from state to state.
- ❶ **Due Diligence fee.** This is different from Earnest Money (see next bullet point). It is a nonrefundable fee offered by the buyer as a demonstration of goodwill; the dollar amount will vary, depending mostly on what has become customary in your area. The Due Diligence fee demonstrates to you, the seller, that the buyer is serious and is not wasting your time. This fee is delivered in a check made out to you directly and is

nonrefundable, even if the buyer walks away. If the purchase goes through, this fee is applied to the sale price.

ℹ️ **Earnest Money.** This refers to a deposit presented with the purchase contract, in order to demonstrate that the buyer is earnest. Unlike the Due Diligence fee, this deposit is held in a trust or escrow account until closing. It is fully refundable to the buyer, without penalty, if the buyer chooses to terminate the contract for any reason prior to the end of the Due Diligence period. The amount offered will vary significantly—usually between 1% and 10% of the sale price. It is applied to the sale price at closing.

ℹ️ **Termination Time.** If a buyer does not terminate the contract before the time specified (usually either 5 pm or midnight) on the last day of the Due Diligence period, the Earnest Money becomes automatically committed to the purchase and is nonrefundable. The only way a buyer can recover their Earnest Money after the Due Diligence period has ended is by negotiating with the seller to release all or part of it. This negotiation should be handled between attorneys.

ℹ️ **Appliances and Other Movable Property.** This refers to such items that are included in the sale. Make sure that the contract states clearly all items included in the sale that are not "fixtures," such as kitchen appliances, washer and dryer, hot tub, home theater equipment, etc. These are things you are conveying to the buyer at no additional cost. Items being sold at additional cost, such as furniture, should have a separate bill of sale. You might reference that bill of sale in the property contract, itself, but it isn't necessary, and many mortgage lenders require the removal of such references.

❶ **Fixtures Not Included.** Make sure that the contract states clearly all things attached to the property which are not included in the sale, such as chandeliers, wall sconces, mirrors, or shelf units fixed to the wall. You will remove these before the closing. If the new owner arrives to find lighting fixtures or appliances removed that they believed were part of the sale, you can imagine how upset they might be.

❶ **Settlement Date and Grace Period.** The settlement date, or closing date, is the Big Day—when you get paid and the new owners get the keys to your home. Most sales contracts include a clause allowing for a grace period, which enables either party to extend the closing date for a set period with no penalty. The period varies by state, and can be up to 14 days. Most sales close on time, and mortgage lenders do their best to get everything ready so as not to hold up the closing, but unexpected events do occur. If either the buyer or the seller has to use the grace period, all that is normally required is to let the other party know the new closing date as early as possible.

• **Special Arrangements** for transfer of possession.

> *Seller possession after closing.* Occasionally, for a variety of reasons, a seller may need to stay in their house for a short period after the closing date. Most state real estate commissions provide a legal document that does a pretty good job of protecting both buyer and seller from liability in this situation. Decide in advance if this may be an issue for you. If you try to negotiate it later, you are not in a strong position as you have already entered into a

contract that doesn't include it. Be aware that it may be a deal-breaker for the buyer. If the buyer does agree, you may have to offer some kind of compensation.

Buyer possession before closing. This is much less common and involves more potential risk and liability. Most state real estate commissions can supply a document for this scenario as well.

Consult your real estate attorney before agreeing to either of these addenda. He or she may suggest enhancing the wording to increase your level of protection.

CHAPTER 12

The Closing

Additional Costs

Your agent and attorney will advise you on what closing costs you will have to pay. Closing costs vary from state to state. They are usually deducted before the money reaches your bank account and may include:

- The real estate agent's commission.
- Paying off your mortgage, home equity loan, or any other outstanding liens on your property.
- Excise tax or other state levy (usually paid by the seller, though this is sometimes negotiable).
- Proration of property taxes (depending on whether taxes have been paid or remain unpaid, a sum of money will be adjusted from the closing proceeds so that seller and buyer pay the portion of the year's taxes that matches their corresponding ownership of the property).
- Proration of Home Owners Association (HOA) dues—if the property lies within an HOA—and any transfer fees.

Seller Courtesy Document

A week or two before closing, provide the buyer with a list of any information that would benefit them as they move into your home: this is known as a Seller Courtesy document. It should include names and phone numbers of all the companies and people who provide services for your home: utilities (gas, water, electricity, garbage collection and recycling services, etc.), cable and Internet providers, security system, yard services or landscaper, hot tub or pool service, handyperson, electrician, plumber, and perhaps your neighbors.

Leave your home well cleaned and your lawn and garden mowed and beautiful. A vase of flowers and a note saying "Welcome home" is a particularly pleasant touch. On the note, let the new owners know where appliance manuals are located, as well as garage door openers and extra keys.

You might even go a bit beyond. For one home I owned and sold, I paid my gardener to return and cut the grass once more 10 days after closing, knowing that the buyer did not arrive owning a lawn mower. It cost me $50, and the buyer was surprised and grateful, and felt welcomed to the community.

Good karma will come to you if you do these things!

Part Four

DIGGING DEEPER

CHAPTER 13

Foreclosure and Bankruptcy

I have faced foreclosure. I have been through bankruptcy. I have had to sell my dream home in a short sale. I understand these issues, not only as a real estate agent but as someone who has been through them myself.

When the economy crashed in 2008, I did not see it coming. Flipping properties for profit was all the rage at that time, and I had invested a lot in real estate. I bought properties that were well-priced and spent money on them to enhance their value. Suddenly, I had to sell everything, and I had to do so at a loss. Eventually, I had no choice other than to file bankruptcy.

I was devastated. I felt like a failure. I had destroyed my family's security.

I was desperate to get my family to a safe place, so we left our dream home and rented a house for much less than the mortgage amount we were paying. After three months, I realized that our old home was just sitting there empty and closed up. Weeds were taking over the yard, and the house itself was degrading. The price it would sell for was dropping with every day that passed. I had run away, and now I saw that what I had done was insane. But nobody told me, "Don't do that."

So, I will tell you: don't run away. Before you make any decision, stop. Take the emotion out of the decision-making process. Don't overreact from a place of panic or shame.

In the end, everything is going to be okay. You will go through a process that many others have survived, and you will come out the other side. It will not break you unless you allow yourself to be broken. Hopefully, you will lose neither your health nor the people you love. You may lose some possessions, but remind yourself you can buy new things, and a new home, when you are back on your feet again.

The moment you find yourself struggling to make your mortgage payments, stop and assess the situation. Ask yourself, "Is this a very temporary issue or will this persist?" Resist the urge to reach into your savings or retirement accounts, or your children's college fund, just to keep things going for another month. DO NOT squander your family's financial safety net. Yes, you are facing the threat of foreclosure if you don't pay your mortgage. But if you catch yourself in time and do what needs to be done, you can still hold on to your savings.

As soon as possible, meet with an attorney who specializes in bankruptcy. Don't be embarrassed or fearful. This is merely a conversation to explore the options available to you. Bankruptcy attorneys are usually kind, compassionate people who are there to help you.

Foreclosure

Foreclosure is a legal process in which a lender attempts to recover the balance of a loan from a borrower who has stopped making loan payments by forcing the sale of the asset used as the collateral for the loan.

In foreclosure, your mortgage holder takes control of your home. They will turn around and sell it for as much as they can—but all they care about is getting their loan repaid. You may have equity in the property above the amount of the mortgage, but the mortgage holder doesn't care about that. The mortgage holder controls the situation, and they have no incentive to sell the property for any more than the value of the outstanding loan. Consequently, they may sell your house for far less than its market value.

The day of foreclosure is the day the lender files the foreclosure in court. The day the foreclosure judgement is executed is the day the property is sold at auction to the highest bidder. It's painful for a family, and even more painful for the individual who is the family's breadwinner, to face the prospect of losing a home to foreclosure. Not to mention, by the time you've reached this point, you've suffered shocking, destabilizing life experiences.

It's tempting to delay facing reality and hope desperately that things will improve. It's tough to draw a line under this chapter of your life—especially if it's your dream home that you're about to lose. But the sooner you make this hard decision, the better it will be in the end.

Assess your individual situation. If you can no longer meet your mortgage payments, and cannot realistically see your situation improving soon, you must act. Meet with a bankruptcy attorney immediately and explore your options. Don't put this off. The sooner you take steps, the better off you will be. You may be able to stay in your home for many months while you're moving through the bankruptcy process or until you achieve a short sale (see below). I know of people who were able to stay in their homes for two years without making a mortgage payment during the post-2008 recession. It all depends on the value of the property, how difficult it is to sell, the amount of the outstanding loan, and what's happening internally with your mortgage holder.

But the basic rule is: if you cannot make your mortgage payments, you need to sell your house. You need to get as much money as you can from it, rather than losing everything. You need to keep control of the process. Protect yourself from foreclosure while you still can. Find yourself a good broker, go through the process of letting go described in Chapter 15 "Energy, Intention, and Intuition," and list your home for sale.

Short sales

When the property market falls, some home owners will owe more on their property than it is currently worth. This is referred to as being upside down in your mortgage. In this situation, you have two choices:

1. **Sell the property and absorb the financial impact.** Let's say you owe $470,000 on your mortgage. Even though you paid more than that for your property, the best price you can get for it now is $400,000. You can accept the offer, give all the money to the mortgage holder, and write an additional check for $70,000. This will get you out of debt, and your credit will remain intact. Of course, not everyone can afford to do this.

2. **Ask your mortgage holder if they will accept a short sale.** This is the more common solution. If you are upside down, it's likely that you're not the only one in your market. The mortgage holder holds other mortgages, so they will understand that the property market has fallen. They may understand that they are unlikely to get the full amount of the loan repaid and agree to accept less than what you owe to cancel the mortgage and release you of the remaining debt, writing off the difference as a business loss. The alternative is that they will file a "deficiency judgment" against you, ordering you to repay the difference. During the difficult years of 2009-2013, some states passed laws prohibiting lenders from pursuing deficiencies from short sales. These laws forced mortgage holders to write off those losses.

Ask your attorney or research the laws in your state before you open negotiations with your mortgage holder. Even if your state does not prohibit lenders from pursuing deficiencies, ask your mortgage holder if they will accept a short sale.

You will need to negotiate with your mortgage holder and deal with any legal documents—this is not something that a broker can do for you. Agents are not allowed to practice law, so they are careful not to give legal advice or perform tasks that could be construed as acting as an attorney, such as creating or facilitating legal documents. Whether or not the situation is complicated, hire an attorney. Having good legal representation is worth every cent.

You will certainly need a real estate agent to handle the sale. There are many nuances to consider in short sales, and these vary from state to state, so find a real estate agent with experience in short sales. Identify two or three, meet with them, and ask them how they can help you. Ask if you can talk to any previous clients who were in a similar predicament. Choose the broker who you feel has the most experience in successfully handling short sales.

As you consider the sale price that the broker recommends, remember that real estate brokers, in their desire to get a listing, may lead you to believe that your property is worth more than it really is. Don't just take their word. As I advised earlier, ask for the information they used to arrive at the figure they gave you and examine it yourself. Assess honestly whether your home is worth more or less than the properties the broker has used for comparison. Remember, a property that hasn't yet sold may not be worth the price it's currently listed at. It's vital, before you open discussions with your mortgage holder, that you have a realistic idea of the likely sale price of your home.

Bankruptcy

You have hit financial hard times. Your income has dried up, you are behind on your mortgage payments, and other bills are piling up. You have even put your house on the market, but no buyers are showing up. You cannot see your way out of the situation.

Sit down with a bankruptcy attorney right away. There's no question this is heartbreaking, but act intelligently, and don't let your emotions control you. In our culture, most of us are raised to see bankruptcy as a terrible human failing. Yet in 2009, over 1.3 million individual non-business bankruptcies were filed in the U.S. For the period 2009 to 2012, there were more than 5 million. In 2020, due to the corona virus pandemic, the number is expected to exceed 5 million. It's important to forgive yourself for having arrived at this point. If you are fortunate, your loved ones will understand and will endure these tough times with you.

IMPORTANT: Retirement accounts are protected from creditors and from tax authorities, so don't make the mistake that I did, that of cleaning out your savings before you take this step. As soon as you file for bankruptcy, all foreclosure proceedings must cease and no new proceedings can commence. This "automatic stay" remains in effect until the bankruptcy judge approves your bankruptcy. Meanwhile, you are normally allowed to stay in your home. Even though you are not making monthly mortgage payments, your mortgage holder knows that an empty house deteriorates fast. The building fabric crumbles. The landscaping goes to seed. There may even be vandalism. Most mortgage holders are aware that they are better served by allowing you to stay in your home and care for it.

CHAPTER 14

How to Fire Your Real Estate Broker

What if your home has been on the market for a year and it still hasn't sold? If you did your homework at the beginning, you have chosen a good real estate agent. If you feel that your broker is doing all the right things, there's no reason to move on to someone else.

Sometimes it just takes that long to sell a property. High-priced luxury homes typically take longer to sell, as there are fewer buyers in that price range. Perhaps your price is too high, and you need to drop it. Maybe some aspects of your home are turning buyers off—you know about these through the feedback from buyer's brokers. If you haven't dealt with these, that's your fault; you could have repainted that bright yellow living room in a more neutral color, or repaired the deck. If the problem can't be dealt with, it's not the real estate broker's fault either.

But what if you feel your agent is not doing an adequate job? If the listing contract has expired, you are free to move on. Even so, you might not want to start all over with someone new, as that's a big undertaking. If there is a possibility of redeeming your relationship and persuading your broker to improve where they have fallen short, I strongly recommend doing this. Have a frank discussion with your current broker first.

If the listing period isn't yet up, you must take control now. You are, for all practical purposes, your real estate broker's boss.

First, communicate your concern. Tell your agent that your expectations are not being met, and explain why. You will be in a stronger position if you added a marketing addendum to the listing contract (see the "Sample Marketing Addendum" at HowToSellYourHomeNow.us) that details your expectations and allows you to be released from the contract if the broker is not fulfilling them. Bring a copy of the contract, including the addendum, to the meeting. Tell the agent that you expect them to live up to the agreement they made with you and ask for a timeline, in writing, for the completion of each item you are requesting they address.

If your agent is understanding of your concerns and agrees to fulfill their contractual obligations, it may make sense to continue the relationship. But don't do this unless you feel that the broker's heart is in it. If they're reluctant to comply with your demands, they will never do a good job of selling your property.

If you did not include a marketing addendum in your listing contract, you might send the agent a copy of this book with a note saying something like, "I've just read this book, and I feel dissatisfied with the work you've been doing on the sale of my home. Please read it, and let's discuss it. I would like to continue working with you, but I want our relationship to change. I hope you will take this the right way."

It's very possible that the real estate broker may respond positively. This is because much of what you have learned in this book is not taught in real estate school. If that's the case, you just helped to change someone's career for the better. Because you stood up for yourself, you've enabled your broker to do a better job for you and for every future client they will have.

If your broker becomes angry or uncommunicative, you have your answer.

Terminating the listing agreement

When you fire your agent, what you are actually doing is releasing yourself from the listing contract. You are in a contractual relationship, so it must be ended by mutual agreement. Most companies have a policy that allows clients to leave, as they don't like the idea of holding a client hostage. They will try to work through the problem with you and find a solution, but ultimately, if you are adamant about terminating, they will probably release you from the contract.

Always try to change the relationship first. See if you can inspire your real estate agent to improve their work. If they don't, they must release you.

Make the request in writing, in either a letter or an email. Later, you may need a paper trail, and an email will suffice. Say something like, "Dear John, I would like to terminate my listing agreement with you effective immediately. Please send me the necessary paperwork for my signature. I look forward to hearing from you promptly. Thank you for your service."

This is an opportunity to be gracious. Your real estate broker has done work and put in time, no matter how unsatisfactory the job might be. Add something like, "I'm sorry for this, but I feel I need to move on. I hope you will honor my choice. I wish you success in the future."

If you don't receive a response within three days, write again.

If you haven't heard back in a week, send another email or letter saying, "This is my third email/letter to you requesting to terminate my listing agreement, and I have not received a reply from you. Again, I would like you to terminate my listing agreement effective immediately. Thank you." This time, copy the agent's boss, who is usually the "qualifying broker" or the manager of that real estate company.

If the agent still does not respond or refuses to release you, write a stronger letter with a copy to your attorney, and a follow-up letter to the head of the agency. A lawsuit brought by a client is very bad PR (public relations) for a company, so this threat will probably bring things to an end. If it doesn't and you have a legitimate complaint, contact the local real estate board and your state's real estate commission. It is extremely unlikely that things will ever reach this point.

CHAPTER 15

Energy, Intention, and Intuition

If you follow the practical advice I've laid out in this book, you have all the tools you need to market your home effectively. However, in addition to this practical information, experience has taught me that there are other important considerations, which are not so tangible. If you find that this approach does not align with your view of reality, feel free to skip this chapter—though if you stick with me, you may find that this material makes unexpected sense. And if you've followed my advice to the letter so far and your home still hasn't sold, the advice I give in this chapter may make the difference.

Energy

Energy is all around us. Everything that exists is alive on an atomic level. The table in your dining room, the painting on your wall, and the walls themselves comprise atomic particles fizzing with electrical impulses invisible to the human eye. They are in constant movement, influenced by the energy of those who inhabit your home.

Imagine going to visit your close friends Jacob and Alicia. Unbeknownst to you, they have just had the worst fight of their twenty-year marriage in their living room. They've left the front door unlocked for you to enter, as they often do. The house is charming as always, but you feel that there's something wrong, as you wait in the living room for them to appear. You feel it but can't explain it. Some people would say that you are sensing the energy of what happened in that room just a short time ago.

Now imagine that you are a potential buyer, viewing a really lovely house. The owners have lived here for fifteen years. They raised a family here. Now they're facing bankruptcy or some other heavy life challenge. Having to put their beloved home on the market is devastating. They are angry: angry at the bank, angry at themselves, angry at the system. They are both embarrassed and depressed.

They aren't present when you visit, and you have no awareness of their situation. You love the décor, the landscaping, the floor plan, the kitchen. But as you walk through the house, you feel unwelcome. You're not comfortable being there. When your broker asks you what you think, you answer, "This house seems to have everything I'm looking for, but I don't know, something just doesn't feel right."

I can't tell you how often I have heard this.

Now, imagine going to a similar house, one whose owners also are forced to sell. But they're making the best of the situation: they're committed to selling their home, and they're focusing their energy on the next phase of their lives.

Your experience in this house will be very different. The owners want you to feel good here, so there's a vase of flowers on the dining table and cookies in the kitchen. Everything is impeccable, looking its best. These owners are not feeling angry or resentful; they want you to buy their home. And maybe you will.

Decades of experience have informed me that homes absorb the energy of the people who live in them. This is not just because gloomy people take less care with cleaning and décor. A home may be immaculate and gorgeous, but if the owners are reluctant to sell it, their unhappiness will be palpable to potential buyers. The vase of flowers won't be there; neither will the cookies. Maybe there will be a vaguely stale smell, or the arrangement of objects on shelves will be careless and haphazard. Maybe the curtains are half-drawn, or the rug isn't straight. These may not be things that potential buyers notice consciously, but even so, they make an impression.

As buyers walk through homes such as those mentioned in the previous paragraph, they may feel a subtle sense of sadness or discomfort. What they'll say, probably, is that they just don't connect. The truth is that they cannot feel that this home could be theirs, because the owners have not yet come to terms with letting it go.

Please don't misunderstand me. I'm not saying you have to be happy in order to achieve a successful sale of your home. You may be selling because of divorce or another difficult life situation. All I'm saying is that you should be clear and unambiguous about your decision to sell your home.

Letting Go

Several years ago, I had a retail business called "A Far Away Place" that sold beautiful items from around the world. In my inventory were some items I loved and didn't really want to sell. But this was a business, and I had to sell them. I would place those objects in the most prominent place in the store, and people would hardly notice them. They would sit there for months, even years. But as soon as I fell out of love with an item—as soon as I tired of it, as soon as my attachment to this item shifted—it would sell. I had let go of the object and people began to see it. This may sound strange to you, but it's true!

The same thing happened with real estate. I once had a beautiful home that the recession of 2009 forced me to sell. It broke my heart: I loved that house, and I felt I was letting my family down. I resisted putting it on the market and virtually bankrupted myself making the mortgage payment every month. Eventually I had to sell the property in a short sale, because I was not willing to deal with the reality of the economy and my emotions earlier.

If you want your home to sell quickly and at a good price, you must come to terms with the fact that you're selling it. You must be at peace with the decision and ready to move on. Your perception must shift. This is no longer your home, but just the place where you're living until you accomplish your goal of turning this asset into the money that will take you forward into the next stage of your life. The important thing now is to handle that transaction correctly, so that the positive effects outweigh the negative.

As the renowned Scottish mountaineer William Hutchison Murray wrote of his attempt to qualify for a 1953 Mount Everest expedition:

> "Until one is committed, there is hesitancy, the chance to draw back, always ineffectiveness. Concerning all acts of initiative and creation, there is one elementary truth... that the moment one definitely commits oneself, then Providence moves too. All sorts of things occur to help one that would never otherwise have occurred..." [This quote is often attributed to Goethe.]

Look honestly at your emotions. Can you transform fear of the unknown into excitement about what might come next? Can you transform anxiety about the future into wonder at how things might unfold? Can you find it in yourself to accept the reality of the situation and do what must be done willingly, with a positive attitude? You don't need me to tell you that, when you have a positive attitude, things often seem to just fall into place.

Sometimes it takes only a subtle shift of perspective. Look back at your life up to this point. I bet you can identify many times when things worked out well in a way that you never expected.

As a broker, this is one of the first things I address in a listing appointment, and it was the question I asked you at the beginning of this book: Are you really, truly ready to sell your home now? If my client says they are not, I work with them on releasing their home, using the techniques I'll outline in the text that follows. Sometimes they say that they are ready to sell but then, after twenty showings and no offers, we discover that a deep-rooted attachment remains unresolved.

Intention

Once you get clear on the fact that you are selling your home, purposefully set your intention. Write it down and say it out loud with clarity and certainty. Then reinforce your stated intention with action.

The mind is a powerful thing, and an entire family coming together and putting everyone's minds on the same thing is even more powerful. When all these minds are working together, deciding what's coming next, it creates excitement. There are no guarantees that anything you plan will actually happen, of course, but planning gets you moving. It changes the energy in the house from resistance to anticipation. It will make you and your family feel more hopeful.

- Involve the entire family
- Spend time looking for your next home
- Start packing
- Use affirmations or prayer to focus your mind

Involve the entire family

If you have a family, you'll need to get them on board. A family meeting is a great place to begin. Include everyone who will be affected by the move.

Dedicate the time and turn off all media. Give everyone a chance to say how they feel about the move, without criticizing or censoring. Have compassion—allow ample time for expressions of sadness and attachment. Then, when appropriate, move the discussion on to the opportunities that the move will create. Make a list of the positive aspects of moving—and make it as long as you can. Challenge one another to think of one more thing. You might come up with items such as:

- A smaller mortgage, which might mean more money for other things
- No home maintenance, because you'll be renting
- A cooler home or neighborhood

- Amazing views
- Walking distance to downtown
- Near a beach, lake, country club or sports park
- A more desirable school district
- A larger yard
- A new pet

Give the kids something to look forward to

It's difficult for children and teens to move to another town or state, or even to another school district. They'll be leaving their friends behind. Acknowledge this. Don't pretend that it isn't tough to start over. But find something positive, an incentive, something that will only happen once the move has taken place. Maybe you'll get a dog, cat, or even a horse. Do whatever you can to get your kids on board. Do your best to make this move an adventure.

Make a vision board

There's an old saying: "If you don't know where you're going and if you don't have a map to get there, how will you ever find your way?"

Get a piece of foam-core board or a pinboard. Put it on the wall and add a title, such as "Our New Life," "Our Future Home," or whatever appeals to you. Now, make some popcorn and get comfortable. Tell your family, "We are going to create our next life. What do we want in our next home?" Urge everyone to contribute their ideas.

What will your dream home look like? Will you have a dog, a yard, a horse? What is the new job going to be like, the new school, new entertainment opportunities, new friendships? Will your new neighborhood have kids playing in the street, or in a park? Will anybody join a baseball team or a football team, play tennis or take ballet lessons? Everybody's opinion counts and no one can be wrong. Even if the opinions are contrary, write everything down.

With all the suggestions written down, now you can create the board. Find pictures of houses and rooms that appeal to you online or in magazines. Put the pictures on the board, in a collage, and down one side list all the things your home will have. Be specific. You might choose things like:

- Large living-room
- Office
- Guest house
- Wood-burning fireplace
- High ceilings
- Great views
- Big kitchen
- An awesome yard
- Playroom for the kids

Fill the board. Encourage everyone to visit it every day. Have fun with this process!

I knew one family who made a vision board and then forgot about it. Two years later, when they moved into a new house, they pulled it out. On the board was a photo of what looked like the exact house they were now living in. They didn't even know they'd done that.

Spend time looking for your new home

Browse the Internet and listings magazines, imagining that one of these homes might one day be yours. If possible, spend time in the neighborhood you plan to move to, looking for real estate agents' signs. If something catches your eye, schedule an appointment to view it, even if you're not yet ready to make an offer.

Take a family trip to the new neighborhood, if possible. Cruise the streets and imagine where you might like to live. Go out for pizza or ice cream. Take the kids to their new school, if appropriate. Do whatever you can to familiarize them with the new neighborhood and show them it's cool.

Start packing

I always encourage sellers, once we have signed the listing contract, to set their intention in motion and begin moving forward with certainty. Packing is a powerful and unambiguous statement that you are moving.

Pack up anything you don't really need for the next few months—even in the kitchen. Keep the boxes open, in a storage area or the garage, and add to them. This will get the energy flowing forward and also declutter your home, making it more attractive to a buyer.

Remove as many personal items as you can. In Chapter 6 "Preparing Your Home for Market," I recommended packing up most family photos and any spiritual, religious, or political items, in order to make your home more neutral and therefore attractive to a wider pool of potential buyers. I'm expanding that advice here to any objects that have an emotional pull and make you look back instead of forward. Objects with strong emotional pull are focuses of attachment, and if you are not seeing them in your home, you'll find it easier to detach.

But don't get too carried away! Remember that your home should still feel like a home when potential buyers come to view it.

Use affirmations and prayer to focus your mind

When you verbalize the plan you've decided upon and the outcome you desire, you keep your mind focused on the positive and the future. You corral your wilder thoughts. You calm anxiety and doubt. If you find yourself slipping back into uncertainty or unwillingness to sell your home, try using prayer, or if you are not a religious person, affirmations, to get yourself back on track. Gratitude and generosity are helpful in bolstering your positive state of mind around the entire experience.

The prayer or affirmation can be short. The most important thing is that you commit to it whole-heartedly with the desire that your home sells.

A prayer—to God, the Higher Power, or the universe—might go
something like this:

> "Thank you for providing us this home. It is time for us to
> leave here now, and we are ready to go. Please bring us
> someone who will purchase and enjoy this home, so we
> can move forward with our life."

An affirmation might sound something like:

> "I love this home and I release it to its new owners,
> wishing them love, peace, and happiness here."

If you do this each time you prepare your home for a viewing,
you'll feel energized to make your home as attractive as possible.
Make it feel warm and welcoming to the potential buyer.

Of course, I can't guarantee that doing this will bring you an
offer within a week. What I can assure you is that preparation
like this brings momentum to the process of selling your home.
You'll feel more hopeful. You'll feel excitement and anticipation.
Your home will be more attractive to potential buyers because
you may have done things like:

- Given your home an extra-thorough cleaning
- Opened all curtains and arranged them nicely
- Adjusted the heating or air conditioning to a
  comfortable temperature
- Turned on all lights if it's a dull day, or evening
- Left a plate of cookies on the kitchen counter
- Set out at least one vase of fresh flowers
- Raked up the dead leaves and/or pulled the weeds
- Left a note welcoming the potential buyers to
  your home

There are many situations in life that we can't control, and
this may be one of them. But even if you can't control the
situation, you can put conscious intention on how you respond
to it. I promise you, this will influence the outcome.

The Saint Joseph statue

Many people use a small statue of Saint Joseph and the Saint Joseph Prayer to help them sell their home. These statues are widely available online, and come with a few different prayers and varying instructions—often, to bury the statue upside down near the front of your home.

There are countless stories of people who have done this and had their home go under contract very quickly. There are also many stories of people who followed the instructions to a T, with no results.

If it feels good to you, performing a ceremony with an icon or physical object can be very helpful in setting your intention. You might add a prayer and even an offering as an expression of gratitude. Once you have hired a great broker and set your price, find an object that is meaningful or even sacred to you. Sit around the table with everyone affected by the move and say your prayer, then take the object to a special place of your choosing and leave it there until you sell your home. As you do this, make an offering: a gift or promise to your church or to a special cause in your community.

Still, whether it's a Saint Joseph figurine or some other sacred object that you bury in the earth or place on your mantel, the success of the ceremony will depend on multiple factors: the purity of intention accompanying your ceremony (because that expresses your commitment to the sale), and also more mundane considerations such as your price and your marketing. If you price your home 20% above its market value, it is highly unlikely that even Saint Joseph will be able to help you.

Moving because of financial difficulty

It's hard to feel good about downsizing because of financial difficulty. How can you make this experience more positive?

First, be glad that you are taking steps to remedy the situation. Just because you are experiencing hard times right now doesn't mean that times will always be hard. I love the song "Todo Cambia," or "Everything Changes," by the Argentinian folk singer Mercedes Sosa. Remind yourself that everything in life is always changing, and, although change may be difficult, it always brings new possibilities.

You might still choose to make a vision board of everything you want in a new home, while understanding that this isn't realistically your next step. It's a destination: the goal of a journey. Like any journey, this one requires a map.

Even if the dream house seems impossible right now, consider what a realistic next step might be. Explain to your family that this is a step toward the dream house. Go through the process as I explained it earlier, asking one another what things are truly essential to creating a good life for your family. You might come up with list items like:

- The family coming together every evening to share what's happened during the day
- A pet
- Good health
- Good food
- A nice yard
- Good friends
- A good job

Find images that express those items: a kitchen table with enough chairs for everyone, places to walk or exercise or hike, the food you will buy.

It can also be helpful to expose your family to the experiences of others who are having an even harder time. Perhaps watch a movie together where a person or family goes through a tough time and makes it through to a better life—something to give you and your family perspective. Things will change. Life will be better again soon.

Intuition

Intuition is the ability to feel and understand something immediately, without conscious reasoning. Some people describe it as "listening to their inner voice."

In his book *Blink: The Power of Thinking Without Thinking*, Malcolm Gladwell discusses our subconscious ability to pick up on information while drawing on past experience. In doing so, we can gain a feeling we may not be able to explain, or we can arrive at knowledge with a certainty other people cannot understand. Imagine, for example, a mother who knows her child is getting sick before any symptoms appear. Or a soldier who dives to the ground a millisecond before the shot that would have killed him. Or thinking of someone you haven't spoken to in a long time right before the phone rings, and it's them.

If you're a spiritual person, you might describe this as being guided by God, or angels, or the universe. It doesn't really matter how you define it. The important thing is to acknowledge this inner voice and honor it. That does not mean we should follow it blindly. Question it, dissect it, try to understand it if you can. Just don't ignore it!

Yes, this is a business transaction which requires grounded, logical processing. But we don't always make our best decisions by using only rational thinking—and sometimes we can take all the rational arguments into account and still be undecided. Sometimes you just have to feel what's the right thing to do. This is not being weak, or too emotional, or irrational: it's allowing your unconscious competence to help you.

As you move through the process of selling your home, if something does not feel right, put things on pause for a moment. If you wake up in the morning with a doubt you didn't have before you went to bed, pay attention to it. Whatever the doubt or reservation is, ponder it. Maybe this agent, who seems so competent, is not the right person for you because your personalities will eventually clash or because his or her principles differ from yours. Maybe the photo, or the description, that your real estate broker is pressing you to go with doesn't showcase the one thing that the right buyer will fall in love with. Trust your intuition!

After reading this book, you can be confident that your intuition is based on extensive knowledge of how to market your home. Your unconscious competence is vastly greater than it used to be. You may not have sold a home before; you may not have taken such an active part in the process, but now you have enough information to make quick decisions with confidence. There are many visible, tangible aspects of selling your home—and there are invisible, intangible aspects as well. In order to get the best price possible, you must capitalize on both. If you don't want to undersell your home, don't undersell yourself.

Leaving Your Home as a Gift to the New Owner

When you're finally ready to say goodbye to your old home for good, you have a choice. You can just remove your stuff and hit the road, knowing you will never see the people who have bought it again. Or you can be generous and make the property welcoming for its new owners. That may be hard, if a difficult situation has forced you to sell. Still, I have learned that when you are generous in everything you do, even when things don't feel fair, the goodwill comes back to you. And even if it doesn't come back to you, the experience of leaving your home will be more positive if you infuse it with love and care.

I highly recommend that you take the time, when you are leaving your home, to make it a sacred process. You are delivering to someone else the vessel that has sheltered and nurtured you and your family, that has given you enjoyment and comfort. Consider leaving this vessel polished and bright for the next people to use it. They will feel blessed and grateful, and you will know that you gave them a beautiful gift.

Doing this brings this chapter of your life to a positive close. It will help you feel good about moving on to the next step in your journey.

Thank you for hanging in here with me. I hope this book has helped to demystify this process for you and given you all the tools you need to sell your home intelligently, hopefully making a little more money and most of all enjoying the ride!

Happy travels!

About the Author

Mark Fields was born into the world of real estate. As a young child in the Bahamas, he grew up watching his father operate the islands' largest real estate brokerage.

Later, as a young man, he joined his father's tourism and real estate businesses in Costa Rica, where he eventually opened his own real estate company.

He returned to the U.S. in 1990 and worked in conservation education while brokering large ranches in Central and South America to conservation-oriented investors.

In 2008, he obtained his U.S. real estate license and began working as a licensed broker specializing in luxury properties in Asheville, North Carolina. Throughout his career he has brokered over $200 million in sales. He is a member of the National Association of Realtors.

Mark is currently working on three accompanying books: *How to Buy Your Home Now, for the Best Price Possible; Should I Fire My Realtor or Bake 'Em a Cake?;* and *How to Be the Best Realtor in the World.*

Visit HowToSellYourHomeNow.us for further resources about selling a home.

Online Resources for Selling Your Home

Resources available at HowToSellYourHomeNow.us

- ❶ Real estate broker interview checklist
- ❶ Sample marketing addendum
- ❶ Broker's commission table
- ❶ Photography/ home showing preparation checklist
- ❶ Sample marketing materials
- ❶ Photography, interior and exterior
- ❶ Titles
- ❶ Descriptions
- ❶ Features list
- ❶ Websites
- ❶ Broker e-blasts
- ❶ Home colors that sell, interior and exterior
- ❶ Lighting fixtures that sell homes
- ❶ Lighting: types of bulbs
- ❶ Landscape lighting
- ❶ Staging your home, before and after photos
- ❶ Sample seller courtesy document
- ❶ Sample "seller possession after sale" document
- ❶ Sample "buyer possession before sale" document
- ❶ Sample affirmations
- ❶ Sample vision boards

www.ingramcontent.com/pod-product-compliance
Lightning Source LLC
Chambersburg PA
CBHW060043210326
41520CB00009B/1242